KATE HIGGINS blogs at A Burdz Eye View (
She has spent the last 15 years working w
charities, engaging with political institutior
grew up with politics ever present in her c
tradition into adulthood, immersing hersel
campaign and helping to co-found Wom
happens on 19 September, she hopes to be able to retire from some aspects of
it all and spend more time with her children and her garden.

Open Scotland is a series which aims to open up debate about the future
of Scotland and do this by challenging the closed nature of many conver-
sations, assumptions and parts of society. It is based on the belief that
the closed Scotland has to be understood, and that this is a prerequisite
for the kind of debate and change society needs to have to challenge the
status quo. It does this in a non-partisan, pluralist and open-minded
manner, which contributes to making the idea of self-government into a
genuine discussion about the prospects and possibilities of social change.

Luath Press is an independently owned and managed book publishing
company based in Scotland, and is not aligned to any political party or
grouping. *Viewpoints* is an occasional series exploring issues of current
and future relevance.

Generation ScotY

Scotland's 20-somethings
– a serious generation for serious times

KATE HIGGINS

Luath Press Limited
EDINBURGH
www.luath.co.uk

First published 2014

ISBN: 978-1-910021-48-4

The paper used in this book is recyclable. It is made from
low chlorine pulps produced in a low energy, low emissions manner
from renewable forests.

Printed and bound by
Bell & Bain Ltd., Glasgow

Typeset in 11 point Sabon
by 3btype.com

Contents

Acknowledgements

The lyrics to Marriage Counselling are reproduced with kind permission of Stanley Odd. (We are big fans in this house and so pleased you gave permission!)

As to everything else, where to begin? Firstly, thanks to Gerry Hassan for asking me to participate in his OpenScotland series. I hope I've added something... Thanks too to everyone at Luath Press for advice and support and actually publishing the thing. To friends and family who helped, critiqued and offered lots of positive support, many thanks. Now all you need to do is buy it...

And mainly a huge thank you to all of Scotland's 20-somethings whose views and voices I've sprinkled liberally throughout. This book really is all about you and I hope I've done you some small justice.

Finally, a thank you to my own 20-something for giving me such a positive reference point for reflecting on this generation. I learned a lot about you from researching this book and appreciate you all the more now. And most especially, to the Boy Wonder who being still at home, put up with it all. Appreciative and understanding beyond your years, maybe one day you'll get around to reading the end result. If your future comes on with just as much sunshine in the bag, I'll be happy.

Introduction

I SPENT MY 20S variously graduating, having a baby, studying for a law degree, getting my first and second jobs, being homeless, buying my first car, beginning and ending three relationships, celebrating my parents' Silver Wedding anniversary, becoming an auntie, losing the last of my grandparents, moving into my first and second rented homes and getting elected as a Councillor.

Yet, in my teens at university, I reckoned the pathway that would define success as an adult would be reaching the seemingly far off age of 30 married, possibly with children, a well-paid job, a decent car and owning my own home. By 30, I had achieved only one of these and probably not in the order that I aspired to.

Looking back, it seems – and it was – an impossibly busy and formative time in my life. And running through it all was the thread of political awareness, of a belief in independence in Scotland, nurtured through formative experiences with my parents, then explored more fully on my own in the 1980s and 1990s.

By the 1990s, my political beliefs and attitudes were pretty fully fledged – they've developed since but are fundamentally the same. And they were shaped not just by that early nurturing but by the torrid 1980s. I subscribed to the *New Statesman* all through my teens; I flirted with Red Wedge (it helped that I liked their music anyway); I sneaked off to a miners' strike picket line to show solidarity and don't think I've ever been so scared since. We marched constantly in that decade: against unemployment, factory closures, service cuts, privatisation, the Poll Tax, nuclear weapons, the Falklands war, US interference in Nicaragua, apartheid, cuts in higher education and against job creation schemes for young people. In fact, there are few things I recall being 'for' in the '80s, other than for better pay and conditions for teachers and for the demise of Margaret Thatcher.

Indeed, this past 12 months have seen the passing of four seminal figures from my youth, all of whom helped shape my understanding of politics in different ways. Thatcher, of course, was the hate figure: every child of '80s Scotland was reared on loathing her. She dominated all matters political and has influenced how we all live our lives today. Mainly, we aspire to be home owners rather than renters; few subscribe to non neo-liberal capitalist economics; most of us have private pensions in some form or another; and like it or not, we might still be community-minded, but we are indeed all individuals now.

Tony Benn was another big political figure for me growing up. In fact, UK politics preoccupied much more in the '80s than they do now, and the fight for the soul of the Labour Party was viewed romantically by a bystander like me. I remember reading the 1983 Labour manifesto and loving every line; I was puzzled by the ridicule and opprobrium heaped upon it by UK media and bemused that the electorate – largely elsewhere on these islands but not exclusively so – rejected it.

The very recent death of Margo MacDonald marks another closed chapter on my formative political years. We mixed in quite different SNP circles when I was a child, but her no-nonsense campaigning zeal, bright and fiery intellect and ability to combine left-wing political aspirations related to class, opportunity and equality with a belief in self-determination were attractive qualities to a gawky and gobby Scottish female teenager.

Lastly, the passing of Nelson Mandela really did seem to mark the passing of an era, prompting a real bout of melancholic introspection. Which global figures of towering political importance, who embody a movement and are capable of capturing the imagination of like-minded individuals all around the world, will be mourned by Generation Y 20 years hence?

This book aims to explore the influences, attitudes and behaviours of 20-something Scots today and to discern what has influenced their political thinking. It won't have escaped their attention that this is the year of the independence referendum. Has this awakened their political appetites? Are they engaged? How do they intend to vote? Is this the much trumpeted 'Independence Generation'?

If we are to understand Scotland's 20-somethings, we also need to know something about them and of them. Who are they? How do they live? Moreover, we need to examine their characteristics within a global context.

Generation Y is a *thing*. The idea of a Generation Y was first posited by Neil Howe and William Strauss in *Generations: the History of America's Future, 1584 to 2069* (Howe and Strauss, 1992). But they used the term 'Millennials' to denote the generation born from 1982 onwards whose lives would straddle and therefore be impacted by two Millennia. So struck were they by how different this generation might be from their parents, the so-called Generation X and Baby Boomers, that they published a separate book in 2000 solely on Millennials:

Over the next decade, the Millennial Generation will entirely recast the image of youth from downbeat and alienated to upbeat and engaged – with potentially seismic consequences for America.

HOWE AND STRAUSS, 2000

The phrase 'Generation Y' was coined later, appropriately enough by the then editor of *Ad Age*, the advertising industry magazine, in 1993 (Crain, 1993). Since then, an astonishing amount of research has been conducted into the habits and mores of this generation and some of the early theories about Generation Y's characteristics have proven hugely influential. But, unsurprisingly, some of these initial theories have also been debunked (Twenge, 2006; Morrison, 2013).

Generation Y and Millennials have also been termed Generation Next, the Net Generation and Echo Boomers, in reference to their parents, who have been termed Baby Boomers. For the purposes of this book, ease of reference and consistency, the term Generation Y is used to describe 20-somethings from any part of the world and Generation ScotY (pronounced Scotty, natch) for those 20-somethings who currently live in Scotland but were not necessarily born here.

The first chapter collates what we know about Generation ScotY while the second considers some of the research and theories about their characteristics and attempts to apply these to our own 20-somethings. The last three chapters are devoted to exploring their voting intentions and influences, the role they are playing in the referendum and how they intend to vote on 18 September. Relevant data has been mined, quotes and comments purloined so that the voice of Generation ScotY is heard throughout.

Defining the Generation that Straddles Two Millennia

WHAT AGE DO YOU have to be to qualify as a member of Generation ScotY? Helpfully, there is no one defining demographic, though most agree that the starting birth date is 1982 (Horovitz, 2012; McCrindle, 2012). And while some suggest Generation Y continues right up to the Millennium, most consider its endpoint to be in the 1990s, either 1994 (McCrindle, 2012; Donovan and Finn, 2013) or 1997 (Peters, 2008).

So for the purposes of this book, Gen ScotY is defined as running from 1982 to 1997, with interest focused on, but not confined to, *bona fide* 20-somethings – that is, those who were born between 1985 and 1993:

Born in:	turned 18:	age now:
1985	2003	29
1986	2004	28
1987	2005	27
1988	2006	26
1989	2007	25
1990	2008	24
1991	2009	23
1992	2010	22
1993	2011	21

According to the 2011 Census, there are 363,940 young adults in Scotland aged 20 to 24 and a further 345,632 aged between 25 and 29. Thus, Generation ScotY makes up 13.3 per cent of Scotland's total population (709,572 of 5,295,403 people) (Census, 2011). There are more women than men, in line with general population trends, but the gap does narrow to just over 1,000 in favour of women in the younger age group. Interestingly, there are more Scots in this age group now than there were recorded in the previous Census in 2001.

Scotland is similar in terms of the size of its Generation Y population to other countries. In part, this might explain some of the interest in researching the characteristics of Generation Y: for the first time in two decades, the pool of potential employees, consumers and voters has grown.

Ethnicity and Identity

There is nothing about the accident of birth of being Scottish that I think I can be particularly proud of. We're not somehow better than people who are born in or who live in any other geographically and politically defined population of people. But we're not any worse either.

KIERAN HURLEY

Of the 363,940 young people aged between 20–24 recorded in the 2011 Census as living in Scotland, 336,988 categorised themselves as White. Of these, 82.5 per cent considered themselves to be White: Scottish, with 9.2 per cent considering themselves White: Other British. The next largest group are those who consider themselves White: Polish at 1.9 per cent of the population. Of those who consider themselves not to be White, by far the largest grouping is those who think of themselves as Asian, Asian Scottish or Asian British (20,372) with 2,442 considering themselves African, 600 Caribbean or Black and 1,451 categorising themselves as from Other Ethnic Groups (Census, 2011).

It is a very similar picture among 25–29 year olds: 92.6 per cent of these young adults consider themselves to be White, with 81.3 per cent calling themselves White: Scottish, 7.8 per cent White: Other British and 4.6 per cent considering themselves to be White: Polish. There were 17,475 adults in this age group describing themselves as Asian, Asian Scottish or Asian British, 4,211 as African, 607 as Caribbean or Black and 1,831 as being from Other Ethnic Groups (Census, 2011). Across both age groups, only 774 describe themselves as White: Gypsy/Traveller.

The 2011 Census tells us that even in its young adult population, Scotland is still predominantly White and clearly comfortable with describing itself as White and Scottish. This is borne out by how Generation ScotY describes its identity, demonstrated in the table below:

	Total	Scottish only	Percen-tage	Scottish & British	Percen-tage	British only	Percen-tage
Aged 20–24	363,940	219,425	60	51,143	14	25,832	7
Aged 25–29	345,632	201,123	58	51,122	15	26,245	8

However, these Census findings are only partially reinforced by data from an IPSOS Mori survey into the State of the Nation in 2014, conducted for British Future, and it should be remembered that this data, while only a snapshot on a very small sample size, is much more recent.

This State of the Nation survey shows a significant minority of young adults considering themselves more Scottish, Welsh or English than British, but most respondents considering themselves not just Scottish, Welsh or English but also British:

Identity	16–24	25–34
Sco/Welsh/Eng not British	17	19
More Sco/Welsh/Eng than British	20	13
Equally Sco/Welsh/Eng and British	40	35
More British than Sco/Welsh/Eng	6	8
British not Sco/Welsh/Eng	12	14

Whether it is the different sample size and age range, or whether there has been a shift in attitudes to identity over the last few years, there is clearly a difference. Yet from both datasets, we can draw tentative conclusions, that most of Generation ScotY considers itself to be at least more Scottish than British. However, they are not the only age group to do so and indeed, are not the age group most likely to either.

In the 2011 Census, 20–24 year olds were only fourth most likely to consider themselves solely Scottish, with 25–29 year olds eighth most likely. More of those surveyed in older age groups saw themselves as Scottish only. The same is true to having dual identity (both Scottish and British), although they were also the age groups least likely to think of themselves as solely British, which, as might be expected, the much older age groups are more likely to do.

What the data suggests is that not only is Generation ScotY supremely relaxed about notions of identity, but that it is shifting away from strong notions of Scottishness, despite them being the cohort brought up with a much stronger political sense of everything Scottish.

Living arrangements

It is a shame that YouthLink Scotland has not continued its important surveying of what it is like to 'be young in Scotland' beyond 2009. As a result, there is no up to date research covering the circumstances and attitudes of young adults in Scotland. The report, *Being Young in Scotland 2009* (YouthLink Scotland, 2009), captures important information about Generation ScotY, breaking down findings into two age groups: 11–16 year olds and 17–25 year olds. Given that this book is only interested in information about 20-somethings in Scotland, only the 17–25 data has been considered. And even this carries a health warning: now five years old, it can only provide a snapshot at that time of those at the younger end of the Generation ScotY spectrum.

Yet what it shows is that in 2009, a minority of young adults aged 17–25 lived away from their parents, with 37 per cent living in rented accommodation and only nine per cent owning their own home. Over half (54 per cent) lived with their parents. Given how difficult the financial climate has been for 20-somethings in Scotland (see below) it is unlikely that this has changed much in the last five years.

Indeed, there might even be more of Generation ScotY living with their parents, as Clare Sheppard testifies in her *Open Letter to My Generation*:

> I write this letter to you... from my parents' house, where I live once more at age 25 after five years in my own flat because even working every waking hour across several jobs and saving every penny I can, rent is so high and mortgage deposits are so difficult to save, I can't afford to move back out again...
>
> SHEPPARD, 2014

This experience appears to be borne out by household composition data from the 2011 Census. In 2011, some 139,171 non-dependent children (those over the age of 18) lived in one family with parents who were married or in a same sex civil partnership; 93,358 lived in one family in a lone parent household and 11,937 lived in one family with parents who cohabited.

This means that 244,466 non-dependent children still live with their parents. We can speculate that as these non-dependent children get older, they are less likely to do so, which means that many of Generation ScotY – anything up to approximately a third of them – are living with their parents well into their 20s.

However, we should also note that significant numbers of Generation ScotY continue to establish family units of their own. Although the trend is towards older childbearing, in 2012 18 per cent of all births were born to mothers aged 20 to 24, with 28 per cent being to mothers aged 25 to 29 (National Statistics Scotland, 2013).

Education

The 2011 Census also indicates that 20,928 households comprise only full-time students. In recent years, the number of students in higher education in their 20s has increased (Scottish Funding Council, 2014). In 2003–04, there were 56,795 students aged 18–24, and 28,050 aged 25–29. By 2012–13, this had increased to 70,985 and 33,705 respectively. However, it is not clear from the available data whether all of these students were Scottish domiciled. Figures for Scottish domiciled students suggest that in the last five years, the number of Scottish domiciled students of all ages attending higher education establishments in Scotland have fallen from a high of 215,595 in 2009-10 to 201,600 by 2012–13, a decrease of 6.5 per cent (Scottish Funding Council, 2014). So while it is possible that more of Generation ScotY is in higher education, either full- or part-time, or studying for postgraduate qualifications as well as undergraduate ones, it is not certain that they are.

Employment and unemployment

Dear My Generation,

The generation of low opportunity and lost potential. The generation of four years in university for a part-time job in retail. The generation of working over 40 hours a week (if you're one of the lucky ones) and living with your parents because you STILL can't afford to move out.

SHEPPARD, C

Clare Sheppard of National Collective summarises the overall employment picture for Generation ScotY neatly, if gloomily. Fewer members of Generation ScotY born after 1990 are likely to be found in employment, as a result of the recession. Among Scots aged 18–24, employment has fallen from 303,000 in 2010 to 280,000 in 2013, with falls of 12,000 being experienced by men and women equally. Unemployment in this age group has risen by 4,000 between 2010 and 2013 and the unemployment rate last year was a staggering 18.7 per cent, approximately two and a half times the Scotland wide rate of 7.7 per cent across all age groups (Office of National Statistics, 2014). A Youth Employment Summit hosted by Young Scot and the Scottish Government in 2012 found three groups facing particular challenges: graduates forced to take more non-graduate level jobs; young people with low or no qualifications; and young people with decent qualifications but a lack of available jobs. This last group accounted for some 47,000 young people and had grown by 45 per cent since 2008/09.

The Institute of Fiscal Studies considers that young adults in their 20s across the UK have experienced a disproportionate fall in employment as a result of the recession, compared to the relatively robust employment rates maintained by other ages (Cribb et al, 2013). The experience has been no different in Scotland, and has prompted the Scottish Government to create a Ministerial post for youth skills and employment, the only role of its kind in all UK administrations. This, together with a budgetary focus on creating apprenticeships, training positions and jobs for young adults, appears to have had an impact on reducing rates of unemployment among Generation ScotY since 2011. Even though the figures in employment are still down in 2010, they have started to grow again.

Confusingly, due to the complexity of the welfare system and no doubt also attributable to some of the reforms underway, the number of 18–24 year olds claiming benefits fell from 43,700 in March 2012 to 27,900 in March 2014. Most alarming are the numbers who have been claiming benefits and are therefore economically inactive for long periods. In March 2012, there were 10,000 young adults aged 18–24 who had been claiming benefits for over 12 months and while that had fallen to 4,100 by March 2014, it represented a bigger percentage – 16.1 per cent compared to 11.9 per cent of the total claiming benefits. Worse still, the numbers claiming benefits for over two years have increased, from 500 in March 2012 to 1,900 in March 2014. Overall, the number of 18–24 year olds who are economically active fell from 364,000 in 2010 to 345,000 in 2013 (Labour Force Statistics, 2014).

So possibly not in higher education and also not in employment: clearly some of Generation ScotY are posted missing in action. Though as Young Scot found out at its event on self-employment, there are many involved in their own businesses or self-employed in creative industries:

> For me, I'd like employers to see less obvious transferable skills from stuff that people do in the creative industries.
>
> BARRY McLEAN, Miniature Dinosaurs

However, the employment picture is much brighter for the older part of this cohort. Adults aged 25–34 in Scotland have seen employment increase between 2010 and 2013 by 41,000, unemployment fall by 4,000 in the same period and economic activity increase by 37,000. The unemployment rate is lower even than the national average at 7.6 per cent (compared to 7.7 per cent), yet the worrying trend is the increase in unemployment among women. While it has fallen by 6,000 for men aged 25–34, it has increased by 2,000 for women of the same age (Labour Force Statistics, 2014).

Poverty and inequality

Economically, Generation ScotY has grown up in tumultuous times, experiencing boom and bust in a relatively short space of time, with the impact of the financial crisis which began in 2008 coming to dominate their early adulthood:

Turned 18	Age in 2008	Age now
2003	23	29
2004	22	28
2005	21	27
2006	20	26
2007	19	25
2008	18	24
2009	17	23
2010	16	22
2011	15	21

During this time, household income rose rapidly between 2003 and 2008, but growth in income levels slowed considerably at this point and since 2010, has fallen off a cliff. Young adults have been particularly hard hit:

> Recently, the incomes of young adults have started to fall behind those of the rest of the population. In the immediate pre-recession years between 2001–02 and 2007–08, median income among adults in their 20s did not grow at all. Between 2007–08 and 2011–12, median income among the group fell by an annual average of about three per cent per year – more than for any other group. This is not surprising, given their falling employment rates during and since the recession...
>
> CRIBB, et al, 2013

Meanwhile, poverty and inequality has grown, with young, single adults of working age particularly affected. Since 2007–08, Generation Y across the UK has experienced a sharp spike in income inequality – at a time when it has fallen significantly for older people (Cribb et al, 2013). The Institute of Fiscal Studies refers to research that suggests unemployment in young adulthood can have a detrimental impact on earnings potential and employment prospects in later years. There is also a potential scarring effect for those who set out in their working lives during a recession which can last for up to a decade and which can adversely impact lifetime earning potential. It also remains to be seen how these tough times have impacted on political attitudes among Generation ScotY and whether or not experiencing economic adversity during their 20s influences their voting intentions and behaviours, particularly towards the independence referendum.

The Impact of Technology

But it is also important to note the impact of the boom years on Generation ScotY. As teenagers, they grew up in many cases with access to considerable material wealth in terms of their family homes, holidays, cars, clothes and consumer items. The growth in the last ten years of the availability of devices has also been rapid and they have benefitted from this hugely: not for nothing do some term them 'Digital Natives' (Prensky, 2001), in that they are the first generation to grow up with technology ever present. They feel inherently comfortable utilising the web and technology in every aspect of their lives compared to their parents, who are largely 'Digital Adaptives.'

Thus, in trying to create a picture of the demographics of Generation ScotY, it is important to contextualise their childhood and adolescence social and cultural experiences. Most of Scotland's 20-somethings have grown up with the presence of the internet (the world wide web first went online in 1991). To them, Apple is less of a brand, more of a lifestyle, games consoles are an essential part of many young male adults' lives, and mobile phones ubiquitous for all, with over a third of 16–34 year olds in Scotland living in households with access solely to a mobile telephone (Ofcom, 2013). Audio and visual experiences are largely downloadable, at least since 2005, although the over 25s in particular will have a large DVD collection now gathering dust.

Key music influencers for Generation ScotY include Eminem, Britney Spears, Amy Winehouse, Coldplay and Jay Z. An eclectic mix then, but this is also the generation of reality TV, who scarcely knew *Top of the Pops* and whose Saturday night getting-ready-to-go-out routine has been sound-tracked by *The X-Factor*. They are also the generation who rediscovered cinema, with the rebirth of the animated film through the likes of *The Incredibles and Shrek*; teen movies like *Clueless and Scream*; fantasy series like *Harry Potter* and *The Lord of the Rings*; surprise hits like *Shaun of the Dead and Bend it like Beckham*; and special effects blockbusters like *Avatar* and *28 Days Later*. Thus, we can see how technology has shaped their experiences and tastes.

Many have disparaged Generation Y and anyone who has lived with members of Generation ScotY will empathise with the caricature of its members as Generation Me (*Guardian*, 2014). Yet, while we think we know them, there is surprisingly little research in the UK, never mind in Scotland. Moreover, official data has to be cut and pasted (and different age bandings and definitions somewhat glossed over) to attempt to paint an authentic picture of their defining characteristics.

By gleaning what we have, we have been able to create a partial image of some specific details and it is very much a mixed one. Generation ScotY is effectively of fledgling status, rather than full-blown adulthood. They are a significant group, simply in population terms in Scottish society, not least because for the first time in three generations, they represent an increased working-age cohort. Many of them will have gone to university or college, and some might still be there or have gone back to full-time study, but the option of going to a Scottish university from living in Scotland, particularly from disadvantaged communities, appears to be declining.

Lots of them will have experienced unemployment in recent years and almost all of them will have been hit by lower incomes. A sizeable proportion, willingly or not, can be found living at home with their parents. In their short lives, they have experienced rather spectacular boom in their living standards followed by rapid bust, which shows no sign yet of bottoming out.

Some predict that this will be the first generation to be worse off than their parents, prompting two Generation Y journalists to coin the phrase 'Jilted Generation' (Howker and Malik, 2010). Indeed, an international IPSOS Mori survey found that less than a quarter of Britain's under-30s thought they would have a better life than their parents, prompting the pollster's MD, Bobby Duffy, to comment:

> The assumption of an automatically better future for the next generation is gone in much of the West – and this could have far-reaching implications for how we engage with national and international politics and economics.
>
> IPSOS Mori, 2014

Technology dominates nearly every aspect of their lives and that in itself is fast moving and ever-developing. In many ways, theirs is a very uncertain future, with change a constant and fast moving in all spheres. How does this maelstrom of circumstances influence the political attitudes, views and behaviours of Generation ScotY?

> No-one is paying attention to it, and that's the most upsetting thing. The impacts are going to be huge.
>
> SHIV MALIK

CHAPTER TWO

Considered Useless by Some, But Surely Not for Long?

TRYING TO UNDERSTAND Generation Y and identifying how it behaves has become a significant research topic, particularly in the US. Indeed, it is suggested that similarities and inferences can be drawn from Generation Y's characteristics in North America, Australia and Western Europe (Donovan and Finn, 2013). Consider this map, produced by the Australian sociologist Mark McCrindle, which sets out key characteristics and defining features for each generation. While there are clearly local differences in some of the categories, what is remarkable is how similar and relevant many of these factors are to Scotland and the UK's Generation Y. These will be discussed more fully below.

Different experiences of and attitudes to employment

Understanding how Generation Y differs from other generations in relation to employment needs and interests has been a particular area of study, perhaps because, unlike the previous two generations of 20-somethings, this one is bigger. Given the concern about the need to maintain growing ageing populations in the West from – until now – shrinking working-age populations, the need to recruit and retain from this pool of bright young things has taken on added significance. Moreover, given the shift in demographics and the raising of the retirement age in the UK first to 67 and (in all likelihood) older, young adults today will be expected to work for approximately 50 years. It is unlikely that they will do so in the same way as Generation X, entering a career or vocation for life and staying if not with the same employer, but within similar sectors and doing the same type of work until retirement. Some could even have quite different careers – up to three of 15 years' duration in each does not seem preposterous, given the longevity of their working lives.

Generations Defined

	Builders 1925-1945 Aged 70s - 80s	Baby Boomers 1946-1964 Aged 50s - 60s	Generation X 1965-1979 Aged 30s - 40s	Generation Y 1980-1994 Aged 20s - early 30s	Generation Z 1995-2010 Aged kids - teens
Aust PM's	Robert Menzies John Curtin	Gough Whitlam Malcolm Fraser	Bob Hawke Paul Keating	John Howard Kevin Rudd	Julia Gillard
US President	Truman / Eisenhower	JFK / Nixon	Reagan / GH Bush	Clinton / GW Bush	Barack Obama
Iconic Technology	Radio (wireless) Motor Vehicle Aircraft	TV (56) Audio Cassette (62) Transistor radio (55)	VCR (76) Walkman (79) IBM PC (81)	Internet, Email, SMS DVD (95) Playstation, XBox, iPod	MacBook, iPad Google, Facebook, Twitter Wii, PS3, Android
Music	Jazz Swing Glen Miller Frank Sinatra	Elvis Beatles Rolling Stones Johnny O'Keefe	INXS Nirvana Madonna Midnight Oil	Eminem Britney Spears Puff Daddy Jennifer Lopez	Kanye West Rhianna Justin Bieber Taylor Swift
TV & Movies	Gone With the Wind Clark Gable Advent of TV	Easy Rider The Graduate Colour TV	ET Hey Hey It's Saturday MTV	Titanic Reality TV Pay TV	Avatar 3D Movies Smart TV
Popular Culture	Flair Jeans Roller Skates Mickey Mouse (28)	Roller Blades Mini Skirts Barbie®/Frisbees (59)	Body Piercing Hyper Colour Torn Jeans	Baseball Caps Men's Cosmetics Havaianas	Skinny Jeans V-necks RipSticks
Social Markers/ Landmark Events	Great Depression (30s) Communism World War II (39-45) Darwin Bombing (42) Charles Kingsford Smith	Decimal Currency (66) Neil Armstrong (69) Vietnam War (65-73) Cyclone Tracy (74) National Anthem (74)	Challenger Explodes (86) Haley's Comet (86) Stock Market Crash (87) Berlin Wall (89) Newcastle Earthquake (89)	Thredbo Disaster (97) Columbine Shooting (99) New Millenium September 11 (01) Bali Bombing (02)	Iraq / Afghanistan war Asian Tsunami (04) GFC (08) WikiLeaks Arab Spring (11)
Influencers	Authority Officials	Evidential Experts	Pragmatic Practitioners	Experiential Peers	User-generated Forums
Training Focus	Traditional On-the-job Top-down	Technical Data Evidence	Practical Case studies Applications	Emotional Stories Participative	Multi-modal eLearning Interactive
Learning Format	Formal Instructive	Relaxed Structured	Spontaneous Interactive	Multi-sensory Visual	Student-centric Kinesthetic
Learning Environment	Military style Didactic & disciplined	Classroom style Quiet atmosphere	Round-table style Relaxed ambience	Cafe-Style Music & Multi-modal	Lounge room style Multi-stimulus
Sales & Marketing	Print & radio Persuasive	Mass / Traditional media Above-the-line	Direct / Targeted media Below-the-line	Viral / Electronic Media Through Friends	Interactive campaigns Positive brand association
Purchase Influences	Brand emergence Telling	Brand-loyal Authorities	Brand switches Experts	No Brand Loyalty Friends	Brand evangelism Trends
Financial Values	Long-term saving Cash No credit	Long-term needs Cash Credit	Medium-term Goals Credit savvy Life-stage debt	Short-term wants Credit dependent Life-style debt	Impulse purchases E-Stores Life-long debt
Ideal Leaders	Authoritarian Commanders	Commanding Thinkers	Co-ordinating Doers	Empowering Collaborators	Inspiring Co-creators

mccrindle research | know the times

mccrindle.com.au
1800 TRENDS (1800 873 637)
info@mccrindle.com.au

All of this played a role in PwC Ltd undertaking a global study of its Generation Y employees in 2013:

> A decade after the first Millennials entered the halls of PwC, PwC firms began to notice that the youngest generation of professionals were leaving PwC in growing numbers after just a few years. Additionally, and perhaps even more alarmingly, a significant majority of them appeared to lack interest in the traditional professional services career path, one that required an intense work commitment early in their career in exchange for the chance to make partner later on. PwC knew it needed to clarify the impact of what appeared to be a shift in culture.
>
> DONOVAN AND FINN, 2013

PwC Ltd surveyed not just Generation Y employees, but also Generation X (those in their 30s and 40s). The study found that when you were born made a difference, with Generation X's transactional needs being more dominant in the workplace and Generation Y's social needs being dominant. Generation Y wants to be supported and appreciated, places high value on a cohesive and team-oriented workplace culture and sees being offered and provided with interesting work as key to workplace happiness.

Interestingly, by also surveying Generation Xers, the firm found that its Generation Y employees 'were not alone in wanting greater flexibility at work' and that some of the stereotypes about Generation Y were untrue. They are just as committed to their work as older employees and still value face to face communication over the use of electronic platforms and channels. Yet, ultimately, employees in Generation Y considered excessive work demands worth sacrificing for their personal lives. They want a work-life balance, in other words. PwC made recommendations about how to adapt employment practice to accommodate Generation Y staff: create a flexible workplace culture; fully leverage technology; build a sense of community; increase transparency around compensation, rewards and career decisions; consider introducing or accelerating global mobility programmes; invest time, energy and resources to listen and stay connected to your people; and one size does not fit all.

Some of these 'key learnings' transfer very well in terms of thinking about the needs for Generation ScotY as employees in a domestic setting.

> Young people should learn about responsibilities and other basic life skills, but should bring to the workplace, enthusiasm and the willingness to work.
>
> Scottish Youth Employment summit participant

Young people are underestimated and can bring lots of great things to the workplace! They can offer businesses marketing, many young people are extremely computer literate and are competent at social media and web design and would be great marketing tools for local businesses. Young people also offer a fresh array of ideas, they are more in touch with other young people and so can offer ideas which are relevant and will perhaps redesign a company's opportunity to relate to young people.

Scottish Youth Employment participant

These learnings can also be applied more widely into other areas of life. Are colleges and universities 'fully leveraging technology' in their learning culture? Is there a 'sense of community' in Scottish politics? Do we 'invest time, energy and resources' in listening to what Generation Y has to say? Are there plentiful opportunities for 'global mobility programmes' in degree courses? Is there transparency around 'compensation, rewards and career decisions' in politics and democracy in Scotland and the UK?

Has Generation ScotY got 'sunshine in a bag'?

The initial prompt for PwC's study – that Generation Y staff behaved like workplace butterflies – has echoes in the findings from other studies of Generation Y. When Strauss and Howe conducted their seminal research into Millennials, they predicted that Generation Y would effectively turn its back on some of the behaviours associated with Generation X and become more civic minded, with a strong sense of community, both local and global. But other sociologists have identified a sense of entitlement, increased self-esteem, assertiveness and high expectations (Twenge, 2006) as well as a detachment from traditional institutions and a greater commitment and empathy with experiential peer to peer relationships (Taylor and Keeter, 2010). This has led to Generation Y also being called the Whiny Generation and other less sympathetic epithets.

McCrindle suggests that the financial values of Generation Y are 'short-term wants, credit dependent and lifestyle debt,' yet the Pew Research Centre findings echo those from *Being Young in Scotland*: this generation is highly optimistic about their financial future, even though they have been impacted by the recession. This is largely mirrored in findings from the Prince's Trust research in the UK: only 13 per cent of young people from affluent backgrounds thought they would not get their dream job and only eight per cent didn't feel positive about their future (Prince's Trust, 2011). And again in IPSOS Mori's survey into the State of the Nation for British Future, which found that half of 16–24 year olds were either very or fairly optimistic that 2014 will be a good year for them and over half (53 per cent) of 25–34 year olds thinking the same.

Yet, this optimistic outlook is not universal. The Prince's Trust also identified a '...clear gap in the aspirations of the UK's richest and poorest young people', with young people growing up in poverty four times more likely to think that few or none of their life goals were achievable (Prince's Trust, 2011). Nor do Howker and Malik support the concept of an optimistic Generation Y in the UK in *Jilted Generation:*

> From my middle-class cohort of friends – people who should be doing well – they're delaying having children, having families, settling down. They don't know what to do with their lives. They get personally depressed about this stuff, and it's a quiet depression that happens every day.

Rooted in reality

Is it simply that Generation Y is more pragmatic? IPSOS Mori's State of the Nation 2014 seemed to find so. While resolutely optimistic about their own prospects, Generation Y is much more realistic about Britain's: only around a quarter of both Generation Y age groups were very or fairly optimistic about these. Reinforcing their rootedness in reality – but also perhaps reflecting the financial values and current circumstances of Generation Y – are findings on the key issues facing Britain in 2014. Those aged 18–24 ranked unemployment, the economy and personal finance as the three most important in that order, while 25–34 year olds ranked the economy, immigration and then unemployment and personal finance as the most important (Skinner, 2014).

State of the Nation 2014 also provides insight into what matters to Generation Y, as well as reflecting their anxiety over economic matters. When asked which events in 2014 were important to them personally, the budget was the runaway winner, with just over a third (34 per cent) of 16–24 year olds and 38 per cent of 25–34 year olds saying this was the most important event of the year. And while there were not huge differences with other age groups, there are some surprises there too, particularly the relative importance of the independence referendum to everyone in Britain, including Generation Y:

Which two or three of these events do you think will be most important to you personally?	%	%
	16–24	25–34
The budget	34	38
Football World Cup	26	29
Independence referendum	13	21
Centenary of World War I	13	11
Glasgow Commonwealth Games	9	12
European elections	6	13
None of the above	26	22

Would any of us have predicted that Generation Y in the UK would pick a key political and economic event over a sporting one in terms of being most important to them? Moreover, would any of us have guessed that two out of the top three events of most importance to 20-somethings in 2014 would be political ones? It is only a snapshot, but does point to a greater interest in politics than many would give Generation Y credit for.

More tolerant, more liberal

For many years, IPSOS Mori has also run an Issues Index, surveying every month throughout a given year, and then providing a summary of the index for that year. In 2012 and 2013 the most significant issues for those aged 18–24 and 25–34 have been the economy and unemployment. When looking at IPSOS Mori's Issues Index for April 2014, Generation Y displays remarkably similar political interests to older age groups. Largely, all age groups are concerned about the economy, poverty and inequality, inflation and prices, and the NHS in more or less equal measures.

But the generations differ significantly on three issues:

- Unemployment – over one in five of those aged 18–24 think unemployment is important, compared to just six per cent of those over 65.

- Devolution and constitutional reform – ranks most highly among 18–24 year olds and 25–34 year olds (though overall it is still quite low at a mean of four per cent across these two age groups).

- Immigration/race relations – important to only four per cent of 18–24 year olds and 13 per cent of 25–24 year olds, but seen as most important by 30 per cent of 55–64 year olds. It is worth noting too that while 20 per cent of respondents from England rank this issue as the most important, only nine per cent of respondents from Scotland do.

Research from elsewhere into defining characteristics of Generation Y suggests that 20-somethings have a far more liberal political outlook than older generations, not just in relation to social and cultural issues, but generally being supportive of neo-liberal economic values. These findings would appear to suggest at the very least a significant difference in the importance attached to issues like immigration and race. It is also reflected in attitudes on one key issue – same sex marriage: 'Love shouldn't be classified by gender or sexuality… It just shouldn't matter' – (Shane, LGBT Youth Scotland National Council).

Legislation has now been passed to allow same-sex couples to marry in England, Wales and Scotland. The issue generated a ferocious debate all over the UK and fascinated media commentators and pollsters. A series of surveys undertaken by YouGov shows the stark difference in opinion across the generations. In March 2012, two thirds of 18–24 year olds said they would support same-sex marriage, compared to just over one in five of those over 65. Only eight per cent of 18–24 year olds opposed both civil partnerships and same-sex marriage, compared to 22 per cent of over 65s. A further poll in May 2013 found that nearly three quarters (74 per cent) of 18–24 year olds supported same-sex marriage, compared to only 28 per cent of those aged over 60. Moreover, this was an issue championed by young adults, including here in Scotland, and not just by members of the LGBT community. It prompted the Scottish Youth Parliament to campaign for same-sex marriage under the banner 'Love Equally':

> The Scottish Youth Parliament believes that two people who love each other should be able to get married. The law in Scotland should be changed to allow same-sex couples to marry if they want to do so.
>
> KYLE THORNTON, Member of the Scottish Youth Parliament

This issue emerged as a priority from consultation undertaken by the Scottish Youth Parliament to form a manifesto for the Scottish elections in 2011, in which nearly three quarters of the 42,804 young people who responded to the consultation backed same-sex marriage. Indeed, the Scottish Youth Parliament was one of three key organisations campaigning for the law to change in Scotland, submitting over 24,000 individual responses to the Scottish Government's consultation on the issue and concluding: 'The journey of Love Equally has left us in no doubt that there is an irresistible case for a change in the law to make marriage equality a reality in Scotland.'

The level of interest and involvement in this issue from the Scottish Youth Parliament, which represents young people aged between 14 and 25, is astonishing. The Love Equally campaign engaged tens of thousands of Generation ScotY (and Z) on an issue that they cared passionately about – yet it is probably an issue few would have predicted might fire their imagination. Indeed, while many in Generation X were supportive and over time, public opinion across all the generations appeared to shift more firmly in support of equal marriage, from the outset, Generation ScotY supported it in huge numbers.

When you consider that Generation ScotY is most likely to cite their parents and carers as having the most influence on their attitudes (72 per cent of 17–25 year olds in Being Young in Scotland), and a majority also citing parents and carers as those whom they trust and respect the most, it would appear that other considerations come into play in determining the attitudes of Generation ScotY on key issues which matter to them. The suggestion that Generation Y is simply more socially liberal than their elders appears to carry weight.

Research does appear to demonstrate that Generation Y has distinct characteristics and that those characteristics are shaped by the world in which they have grown up. There are key influences on their attitudes and views, but some of those appear to be contradictory. They might be more aware, more liberal and more committed to equality – 'Everybody has a right to be treated as equal' – but they are just as concerned about economic prospects as older age groups. And while more pessimistic about the UK's economy, they remain largely optimistic about their own prospects in life, which is largely as it should be. Clearly, though, they want the world of work to offer something quite different from their parents' and grandparents' experience. This is the generation that might want to have it all, but would also like everyone to have it all. Its focus on big political and social issues suggests this is a serious generation for serious times.

As the very proud mother of a Generation ScotY member – a son aged 22 – it is interesting to see some familiar traits and some much less so. That is the difficulty with trying to pin homogeneity on a generation – it is made up of individuals, formed and shaped by a wide range of influences and also by their own views and experiences. For example, those from affluent backgrounds (who took part in the Prince's Trust research) are far sunnier on future employment prospects than those from poorer backgrounds: nearly a quarter of the latter think they would end up in a dead-end job and one in five think they would spend some time on benefits at some point in their lives (Prince's Trust, 2011). So, not everyone predicts a bright, happy future for themselves, with the reality of growing up without impinging on aspirations and life chances.

But it is clear that there are trends which Generation ScotY share with their counterparts around the world. This is fundamentally a more liberal generation, both in how it defines itself (Taylor and Skeeter, 2010) and also how it behaves, helping to put issues relating to equality and justice to the top of the political agenda. Is this a consequence of having grown up in a very particular democratic framework and environment? One of the Scottish Parliament's founding principles, after all, is a commitment to open access, enabling young people to engage directly with political influencers and decision makers. Or is it that having democracy 'closer to home' through devolution has played its part in moulding Generation ScotY too, making them more can-do when it comes to influencing opportunities? It remains to be seen how that plays out in terms of voting behaviour and attitudes towards independence.

> We have achieved all this whilst lobbying the Scottish Government on the sidelines, but just imagine the effect we would as young people have if all of the approximated 575,000 18–25 year olds voted in the elections. We could set the political agenda before our campaigns have even begun.
>
> KRIS CHAPMAN, Member of the Scottish Youth Parliament

CHAPTER THREE

Does Generation ScotY Vote Early and Often?

The next few years are going to be exciting in terms of the democratic opportunities arising for the young people of Scotland.

TERRI SMITH, Member of the Scottish Youth Parliament

The background

The oldest of Generation ScotY have only been voting – or at least have been old enough to vote – since 2003. We might think this makes them political novitiates, but such is the nature of our rolling electoral system, it actually means that the oldest might have participated in ten elections – at European, UK, Scottish and local government level. Even those who only turned 18 quite possibly voted in the Scottish elections in 2011 and before we reach the referendum in September, will have had the chance at least to vote in one more election:

Election	2003	2004	2005	2006	2007	2008	2009	2010	2011	2012	2013	2014
Local Government	x				x					x		
Scottish	x				x				x			
UK			x					x				
European		x					x					x

Crucially, most of Generation ScotY will also have had some experience of referenda. Some will be old enough to recall the 1997 referendum on devolution (a few unlucky souls, like my 22-year-old, might even have leafleted for it) and many might have participated in the unsuccessful AV referendum in 2011. Given that previous referenda date from 1979 (devolution) and 1973 (entry to the Common Market), Generation ScotY is approaching this referendum on independence in September with as much experience as the rest of the electorate. This sort of all-nation vote on a key question is therefore not unknown to them and it is a point worth bearing in mind.

In party terms, this generation of Scots voters has only experienced Conservative Government since 2010: their formative political experience has been a predominantly Labour one, at least at UK level. But during their growing up, compared to their parents, there has also been a transfer of focus away from UK politics towards the Scottish sphere. During this time, they have been witness to the rise of the SNP from being a secondary force in Scottish politics to being the primary force. Many of their political opinions will have been formed against a backdrop of change in party political dominance, away from Labour towards the SNP. They have reached young adulthood largely under the auspices of SNP Government in Scotland and the SNP being in charge of running the country is very much the norm experientially.

Yet, research indicates that Generation ScotY is not persuaded by party politics, citing politicians as among the least influential on their attitudes and least respected and trusted (YouthLink Scotland, 2009). This report also found real ambivalence regarding the impact of the Scottish Parliament on their lives, with less than a third of 17–25 year olds indicating that it had made a real difference to life in Scotland. Yet, nearly half of this age group (48 per cent) considered it important to vote and just over half (51 per cent) believed young people to be active citizens.

The perception and reality persists that a majority of Generation ScotY does not vote, yet it is a more informed generation of voters. Modern Studies at Standard Grade and Higher, as well as National Qualifications, became a more mainstream subject choice during the '90s and '00s, meaning that many in Generation ScotY will have studied Scottish devolution as a subject and be knowledgeable about the Scottish Parliament, its powers and its impact. That's the theory, at least.

Do they vote at all?

Recent polling suggests a disengagement from mainstream political activity, with less than half of Generation ScotY indicating that they are certain to vote in the next Scottish Parliamentary elections in 2016:

Likelihood of voting	Percentage certain to vote (10 = certain to vote)		Percentage who will probably vote (8 = probably vote)		Percentage who are undecided about voting (5 = undecided)	
Age	18–24	25–34	18–24	25–34	18–24	25–34
IPSOS Mori June 2012	41	41	11	13	7	12
IPSOS Mori Sept 2013	43	49	14	11	11	15
IPSOS Mori Dec 2013	41	40	11	13	7	12

In the previous chapter, we have seen how Generation ScotY can be passionate about issues that matter to them, such as equal marriage, and are also vexed by the big issues of the day, such as the economy and unemployment. Moreover, there is no indication in these same IPSOS Mori polls that Generation ScotY is setting out not to vote: the figures on 'will not vote' are very low and in some polls, negligible.

18–24 year olds	Consv	Labour	LibDem	SNP	Don't know	Won't vote
IPSOS Mori June 2012	4	36	4	27	18	4
IPSOS Mori May 2013	0	47	9	33	3	1
IPSOS Mori Sept 2013	4	51	4	33	2	0
IPSOS Mori Dec 2013	12	38	4	32	0	0
25–34 year olds						
IPSOS Mori June 2012	5	25	5	39	12	7
IPSOS Mori May 2013	9	40	10	35	10	0
IPSOS Mori Sept 2013	4	36	9	49	1	0
IPSOS Mori Dec 2013	15	45	4	28	8	0

Who does Generation ScotY intend to vote for?

These polls show a gradual but progressive firming up of how Generation ScotY intends to vote at the next elections in 2016. But they also demonstrate trends less likely to be found in other voter age groups in Scotland: a shift towards the Conservatives – perhaps reflecting the neo-liberal economic attitudes suggested by research – as well as considerable ebbing and flowing between the SNP and Scottish Labour. Unlike Generation X and older age groups, Generation ScotY does not seem quite so smitten with the SNP, which is strange, given its historic appeal to younger voters. Long before it was winning elections, the SNP could rely on first-time voters and those in their early 20s to favour them, yet now that it is a successful entity, Generation ScotY seems to be less enthralled.

As we saw in the previous chapter, from Being Young in Scotland, parents and carers are key influencers on the attitudes of Scotland's 20-somethings. Yet the same research also found that friends were also important, with 61 per cent of participants citing them as the biggest influence on their attitudes. McCrindle and Taylor and Skeeter also conclude that peers play a significant role in influencing Generation Y's attitudes:

> Our research has further confirmed that the biggest factor determining the choice a teenager will make is the experiences of their core group of three to eight friends. Rather than making independent decisions based on core values, they live in a culture encouraging them to embrace community values, and to reach consensus.
>
> MCCRINDLE, 2009

This suggests a difference between Generation Y globally and Generation ScotY, with parents and carers playing a bigger role in influencing attitudes. Yet, this influence does not appear to extend fully into voting behaviour.

Parental influence in Scottish parliamentary voting intentions

The pattern of divergence across the generations between Labour and SNP is complex:

	Labour				SNP			
	Jun 12	May 13	Sep 13	Dec 13	Jun 12	May 13	Sep 13	Dec 13
18–24	36	47	51	38	27	33	33	32
25–34	25	40	36	45	39	35	49	28
35–54	28	27	36	30	36	43	38	39
55+	28	36	30	33	33	34	38	37

Generation ScotY is generally more likely to favour voting for Scottish Labour than Generation X (35–54 year olds) and even the Baby Boomers (over 55s). While there is less variance across the age groups in voting intentions for the SNP, the youngest and oldest seem less inclined to support the party of Government. Hop between the generations, and the divergence in intended behaviour becomes more obvious. In most of the IPSOS Mori polls, voters aged 18–24 are more likely to favour Scottish Labour than 35–54 year olds and less likely to choose the SNP. Meanwhile, voters aged 25–34 are not only more predisposed towards Labour, but across most polls, seem inclined to do the opposite of what those aged 55 and over intend to do in relation to the SNP. Even though both age groups move towards the SNP in September 2013, the rise in support from those aged 25–34 is marked, as is the falling away of support three months later. Yet, SNP support remains fairly constant among over 55s.

By considering only one company's polling data over a relatively short period of time is to provide only a snapshot. Add in the variance expressed in voting intentions by some age groups over this compressed time period and it is difficult to reach conclusions. But generally, when it comes to voting intentions for Scotland's two major parties, a difference in generational behaviour can be discerned. Indeed, there appears to be the political equivalent of a gavotte going on across the generations.

Moreover, there also appear to be differences of opinion within Generation ScotY, with those at the youngest end of the age spectrum more likely to favour Labour. If we assume that at least some of this age group's parents will be within the 35–54 age group, we can also see differences between them and *their* parents in terms of voting intentions towards Labour and the SNP. Indeed, the generations seem almost diametrically opposed.

The same is true of those aged 25–34 when compared to those aged 55 and over. If Generation ScotY can be said to be influenced by their parents' voting intentions and habits, it is that they choose to reject them and make their own choices. What might be causing such a generational divide? Well, here are some entirely unscientific musings.

Like all generations before them, Generation ScotY, while influenced by their parents and carers, are generally predisposed to doing what their parents don't do. Call it a generational kickback. The older cohort of Generation ScotY might well be turning its back on the SNP precisely because their parents have found their way to them. For the younger cohort, it is important to note that at extreme ends of the age differential, we are talking about grandchildren and grandparents, who often have a more positive relationship, with respect and understanding seemingly more evident in their interactions. Could it be that as grandchildren, Generation ScotY is more likely to follow the lead of their Baby Boomer grandparents?

Moreover, the SNP is positively mainstream now, which is quite a different proposition from their underdog, anti-establishment status ten years ago. Voting for the party 'out there' might explain the shift among Generation ScotY towards the Conservatives. There might also be a degree of honesty here among Generation ScotY that suggests that even though the SNP has won two successive Scottish elections in 2007 and 2011, it is still not considered to be a lifelong voting habit. Many people voted SNP for the first time in 2011 and it remains to be seen if they now identify with the SNP as their party of choice.

The Conservatives currently have a young, bright, socially liberal leader in Scotland in Ruth Davidson MSP, but then, the number of Generation ScotY MSPs has grown generally. Indeed, more MSPs under 35 were elected than at previous elections, with 13 returned in May 2011 compared to only eight in 2007 (Scottish Parliament Information Centre [SPICE], 2011). The SNP boasts three such members in its Government in Aileen Campbell, Minister for Children and Young People, Humza Yousaf as Minister for External Affairs and Derek McKay, Minister for Local Government. Labour too has promoted some of its bright young things to the front bench, namely Kezia Dugdale, Drew Smith, Jenny Marra and Neil Bibby.

If Generation ScotY needed role models, there are several across the parties to choose from. These younger Labour MSPs and also, Ruth Davidson MSP get as much if not more airtime than older counterparts in their respective parties, while the younger SNP Ministers are competing with

Generation X Ministers such as Nicola Sturgeon, John Swinney and Richard Lochhead. It simply could be that having political role models to identify with is encouraging more of Generation ScotY to consider voting Conservative and Labour.

There is also the factor of freshness. It is worth noting that Generation ScotY will scarcely recall life under a Labour-led administration at Holyrood: they would have been, at most, in their teens between 2003 and 2007. Scottish Labour is largely an unknown quantity in government to Generation ScotY. There is appeal in something new, which is what Scottish Labour represents to this age group.

Given the proximity of the two parties on policy matters, it is difficult to discern the possible attraction of Labour over the SNP, except in two areas. First, Scottish Labour under Johann Lamont's leadership has positioned itself more in favour of targeting support, rather than universalism. Could it be that Generation ScotY, which has borne the brunt of the impact of the financial crisis through unemployment and college cuts, is more inclined to agree with a desire to shift resources away from older generations – the Baby Boomers and Generation X who have had it all – towards them?

Second, Labour's position on university tuition fees is less definitive and more uncertain than the SNP's, which has made free university tuition something of a totem policy. Labour has flirted with the idea of tuition fees and certainly the party at UK level not only introduced them, but continues to support the policy. Why Generation ScotY might be considering voting for a party that would effectively impose a learning tax on almost 50 per cent of its population is perplexing. It is certainly not supported by NUS Scotland, a traditional breeding ground for Labour politicians:

> The idea that introducing charging for university is somehow progressive, when it puts off the poorest students in Scotland, just simply makes no sense. And it would certainly make no sense to the many college students who aspire to go on to university.

> Johann Lamont highlights the priorities of college funding and tackling our poor rates of widening access. And we agree that there must be a focus on educational opportunities for people from the most deprived backgrounds. However tuition fees are not the way to help, and in fact would make things worse.

> ROBIN PARKER, NUS Scotland President in December 2012
> (in response to a Johann Lamont speech)

Whatever the reasons for Generation ScotY having different voting intentions to older generations, we can take heart from the fact that they *do* have different opinions. It would suggest that they are more than capable of making their own minds up with regards to who to vote for, rather than following family tradition. The concept of generational voting, with identity with particular parties being passed down the family, appears to be becoming a thing of the past. That can only be a positive in terms of creating a pluralist, more thoughtful, voter responsive politics.

Why is Generation ScotY less likely to vote?

Fundamentally though, as with young voters elsewhere, Generation ScotY is less likely than other age groups to vote. Why?

> We need change. We need more young voices, poor voices, female voices, non-white voices, LGBT voices, to be heard. For too long, the traditional brand of Westminster politics has been dominated by the rich white straight man, and the rich, comfortable, and powerful don't legislate against their interests.
>
> MAGNUS JAMIESON, National Collective

Research conducted by Matt Henn and Nick Foard suggests that it boils down largely to trust and influence. While first-time voters are engaged and interested, they feel they cannot influence the decision-making process and consider elections as a largely ineffective way of participating in democracy. In short, they are interested but feel marginalised and disempowered. We have known this for years now, with research by the Joseph Rowntree Foundation as far back as 2000 warning not to mistake young people's boredom with politics as apathy (White et al, 2000). Henn and Foard's more recent research simply reinforces such conclusions, as do the views of Kyle Thornton, current Chair of the Scottish Youth Parliament:

> We know that young people are very engaged and interested when they are given the space to talk about the issues they want to talk about. We know from our work... that, YES, many young people are disengaged with politics, but it is the confrontational, party political spin politics that puts them off.

Russell Brand's recent intervention on this issue through a guest editorial spot at the *New Statesman*, in which he explained why he does not vote

– not through apathy but through disillusion with the political class – sparked a vibrant debate, but few answers (Brand, 2013):

> I have never voted. Like most people I am utterly disenchanted by politics. Like most people I regard politicians as frauds and liars and the current political system as nothing more than a bureaucratic means for furthering the augmentation and advantages of economic elites.

His suggestion that what is required is revolution has at least got people, especially Generation Y, which identifies with Brand's views and sentiment, talking about participating in the democratic process. His interview on *Newsnight* has now generated over ten million views; there have been a slew of blogposts – from among others, Catch 21, *Huffington Post* and the New Left Project chewing over what he had to say; and there has also been a lot of chatter in the media, conducted largely by Generation Xers critiquing Brand's right to say anything on this issue at all because he does not vote. Which suggests that the point of what he was saying on behalf of Generation Y was roundly missed.

What needs to change and what might change it?

The large amount of research devoted to why Generation Y does not vote suggests a lot of handwringing on this issue – we know it exists and we know a lot about the reasons for it (Generation Y has been generous in sharing its views), but we are less clear about the solutions. Most agree that the parties themselves need to do more, including Bite the Ballot: 'We are not affiliated to any political party – we think they all need to do more for the youth vote.' But many of the proposed solutions work from within Generation X's comfort zone – education, voter registration and information – and are basic blocks of any and all the campaigns targeted at Generation Y.

The Scottish Youth Parliament's consultation in 2011 supported more of the same, though with an earlier starting point in schools. A resounding 72 per cent of respondents agreed that 'compulsory and good quality political citizenship and democracy education should be provided in all schools in Scotland' and that 'schools should help pupils register to vote' (Scottish Youth Parliament (2011). But Generation ScotY went further in this survey, in which over 40,000 participated, with 70 per cent agreeing that 'election days should be designated as "democracy day" in schools, with opportunities for pupils to explore democracy and watch the voting process if their school is used as a polling station...' Currently, many children and young people are given an additional day off to allow the important business of voting to take place and are expected to stay far away from it, with some particularly zealous officials banning children from being inside polling stations at all.

Given what we know about how Generation Y learns – through experiential peer-to-peer activity – peer-led activity, such as that by the Scottish Youth Parliament, Young Scot and NUS Scotland will make a difference, though the Scottish Youth Parliament's own research suggests the need to start much earlier than when young people reach voting age. Even though these three organisations for young Scots by young Scots are trying to fill the gap, their limited budgets mean even these efforts are fairly threadbare and basic. Young Scot makes some attempt to link the act of voting with the societal rewards and benefits which ensue, but ultimately, what is needed is much bigger change if Generation ScotY is to participate more fully in elections (and indeed, Generation Z and beyond are to be prevented from becoming further estranged from the act and habit of voting).

So far, there has been little inclination by government to harness technology into elections. Generation Y are also Digital Natives, yet little voter information is made available through the platforms they use to access information, such as mobile apps. Can you register to vote digitally? No. Can you vote electronically in Scotland or the UK? No. Until government and institutions offer channels for democratic participation which Generation ScotY use in everyday life, they are unlikely to feel enabled to vote in greater numbers.

The Scottish Youth Parliament's consultation also suggested the need for deep-rooted change: 70 per cent of respondents agreed that 'government has a responsibility to encourage more people to actively participate in politics' and that 'it is particularly important that constituency candidates reflect the people they represent, including women and people from ethnic minority backgrounds.' These findings suggest that rather than staying away from voting through apathy, Generation ScotY might be making a stand, opting out deliberately because the current set-up neither represents their interests nor is representative of their generation.

As Generation ScotY is more likely to be liberal in attitude, more focused on rights, equality and social policy, the issues political parties tend to focus on in elections are likely to be a turn off. There are votes to be won in making a virtue out of policies like equal marriage, more open borders for migration and immigration and even on economic issues as they impact on young adults – an equal minimum wage, more apprenticeships, help onto the housing ladder. Yet, no political party to date appears to have worked out how to straddle the generational divide in terms of enthusing voters of different ages.

The starting point which Henn and Foard identified – a lack of trust among young adult voters – is at the heart of the problem. 'We know that young people find it difficult to relate what has commonly known to be "modern politics," characterised by suits and bitter fights across the floor of parliament and in the national media, to their everyday lives (Kyle Thornton, Chair of the Scottish Youth Parliament). Generation ScotY does not trust the political system, nor does it trust politicians. Yet, turkeys are unlikely to vote for Christmas. The current system suits the political class very well and recent expenses scandals suggest that few lessons about the erosion of trust have been learned; indeed, research suggests that this 'crisis of democracy' is not confined to younger voters (Bromley et al, 2004).

Clare Sheppard, in her 'Open Letter to My Generation,' makes a heartfelt plea to her peers: 'Impotent anger is getting us nowhere. Young voters, we are letting the side down. We're smart. We have so many opinions and so much energy, *let's use it, and let's use it wisely.*' Her view is that Generation ScotY has to vote, to ignore why they feel alienated and to vote to change things from the inside, because rejecting the current system isn't working:

> Because here's the thing, our political system may be rubbish in a lot of ways, but right now it's the only one we've got and ignoring it won't make it go away. If we want something to change, we have to make it change. We have to get involved. Infiltrate the system and work it from the inside. Become such a powerful force and speak with a voice so loud we cannot be ignored and our needs must be met. And the way to do it is laughably easy. We have to vote.

Kyle Thornton takes a different view, seeing organisations that he is involved with as the route to change:

> When we work together, as a collective voice representing young people, we can, and have achieved great things... SYP is more than a charity, it is more than an organisation, it is a movement. It is a collection of young

leaders who are determined to get out into the community and provide a vehicle for young people to have their voices heard, to ensure that those voices are acknowledged and acted upon by decision makers. This is a really powerful idea that goes beyond simply relaying the thoughts of young people. It is about moving beyond traditional party politics, to a type of politics grounded in youth-led decision making, proper engagement with young people, and speaking as a collective voice as we shape our own futures.

Unlike Clare Sheppard, Thornton suggests that the solution to low engagement and interest by Generation ScotY in voting and politics is not through entering and using the system as it is currently configured, but by creating a different kind of politics to challenge the existing hegemony.

For a host of reasons, only part of which can be resolved within the current political set-up, Generation ScotY is less likely to vote in traditional elections. Ultimately, the fundamental issues are being missed, with activity largely addressing the symptoms, rather than the causes of why Generation Y – and Generation ScotY – is less likely to vote. Among those who do vote, there are reassuring signs that they make their own minds up. Even though Generation ScotY is influenced by different issues and political attitudes, parties are proving remarkably resistant, or just wilfully blind, to talking in a language that Generation ScotY understands, on issues which grab its attention. And even though 20-somethings care – passionately – about the economy and the financial climate, many prefer to see them as frivolous and self-obsessed.

Worse, if that were possible, as a society we are effectively excluding them from participation by older generations' refusal to offer multi-media voting channels. Bits of paper and pencil stumps might work for Generation X and Baby Boomers, but they do not for Generation ScotY: by our stubbornness and failure to modernise, we are actively disenfranchising not just this generation, but the generations to come. Which begs the question: which is the selfish and self-obsessed generation, really?

The referendum on independence on 18 September has been styled as a debate about Scotland's future and within that debate, many versions and visions for that future are emerging, some of them from within the current constitutional set-up, others forming a blueprint for creating a new country and society and therefore predicated on Scotland voting Yes. Does it then follow that a generation that largely rejects the established ways of doing things is enthused and engaged by this great debate? Does the referendum offer hope to Generation ScotY? Is it seeing an opportunity to sweep away all the barriers to political engagement? Does it sense the chance to put its issues – the causes that matter to them – front and central? Are Scotland's 20-somethings involved at all, or are they greeting it all with an ambivalent shrug of the shoulder?

CHAPTER FOUR

Is Generation ScotY Leaving the Cage?

We're living history right now. There's a real buzz around Scotland and that's only going to build as we get closer to September.

ANDREW REDMOND BARR, National Collective

THE REFERENDUM ON independence for Scotland has witnessed and may even have enabled the flourishing of Generation ScotY's engagement with politics.

First, there are the official campaigns. Better Together, the campaign for a No vote and for Scotland to stay within the United Kingdom, has youth reps, made up of young people aged between 15 and 21.

Its launch photo suggests that it has had some success in attracting young people from across the main parties campaigning for a No vote – Conservatives, Scottish Labour and Liberal Democrats – as well as those with no party affiliation. Their views are encapsulated in this blog post:

> In an increasingly globalised world, the internet, culture and social media increasingly blurs traditional boundaries. Young people are at the forefront of this by sharing ideas and a culture that is bigger than parochial nationalism. It is young people in Scotland who are the first to embrace the fact that their world doesn't have to stop with the Borders. That's why me, my friends and so many other young people across Scotland will be saying no to separation in 2014.
>
> O'SHEA, 2013

The official 'Best of Both Worlds' video features young voices as well as 20-somethings setting out their views about Scotland. There's also a video featuring only Generation ScotY giving their reasons for voting No to independence:

> We get the best of both worlds... 60 million people working together as a family... more jobs and opportunities... now is not the time... we need to increase opportunities we have, not decrease them... we will have

more opportunity if we stick together... what makes us so different we need to put up a border?

On the pro-independence side, there is an official Generation Yes part to the Yes Scotland campaign which works for a Yes vote in the referendum. Yes Scotland was much slower off the mark to establish a 'youth wing' for its campaign, but the launch claimed its intention to create 'the largest youth movement Scotland has ever seen.'

Like Better Together, Generation Yes has videos, blog posts and social media platforms to reach its audience. But both seem a bit cobbled. The messaging on Better Together videos mirrors that of the official campaign, utilising all the key phrases that pepper leaders' speeches and stock materials. And Generation Yes cannot decide if it is that or Yes Youth and Students; at the date of writing, it had few materials available and no events showing on its calendar. It all seems a little last minute (it was only launched in March 2014), though with bright young things like David Linden and Miriam Brett at its helm, with resources, it might well come good.

There are also members of Generation ScotY employed at the heart of both campaigns: Gail Lythgoe at Yes Scotland and Rob Murray at Better Together, both of whom are only just in their mid-20s, as well as a host of interns and volunteers turning up at both doors looking to help out.

Generation ScotY grassroots involvement

To find the real flourishing of Generation ScotY in this referendum campaign requires looking away from the official camps to the ones which have, literally, sprung up in response to the referendum. Perhaps the best example is National Collective, a collective of artists and creatives supporting independence. Mainly – though definitely not exclusively – young, many of its members are Generation ScotY and it now has over 2,000 members, with local groups in each of the six cities. National Collective harnesses a range of media and platforms to explore what Independence means – writing, video, cartoons, poetry, drama, visual art and performance. It puts on events, has produced films and invites people to post their wishes for the future. It has a democratic, collaborative, participatory feel to its activity, with no one setting rules and guidelines and all free to contribute. Its Yestival run over early summer 2014 summed up its approach and ethos:

Yestival seems to be a great opportunity to showcase Scotland's contemporary musicians, writers and artists and to maintain that strong artist perspective to the independence debate. That the tour is travelling across Scotland's diverse and vibrant communities – urban, rural and island alike – is a story in itself.

JULIE FOWLIS

The Radical Independence Campaign (RIC) is another grassroots movement that has emerged to campaign for a Yes vote. While it was formed largely by stalwarts of Scottish left-wing politics, it has attracted 20-somethings, with many getting involved in its events and canvassing activity. RIC has hosted lectures, produced a book and hosted an annual conference. Its leadership appears male-dominated, though at grassroots level, its activity appeals to women, creating an inclusive, diverse and egalitarian community approach.

There are fewer such grassroots adjuncts to Better Together, but what they appear to have been more successful at is reaching Generation ScotY audiences with their messaging, although any linking between polling and the impact of any of the official campaigns can only be tenuous.

Let a thousand Generation ScotY flowers bloom

Ripples from the referendum extend even further, with a host of completely independent voices appearing, particularly bloggers posting their views, experiences and thoughts. There's the Science of Independence, the blog of a '20-something research scientist from Glasgow, finally getting round to typing my ramblings up and inflicting them upon the unsuspecting folk of the internet', and Bright Green Scotland, a collective of mostly 20-something Scottish Green activists who focus on environmental and social justice issues and have lots to contribute relating to independence issues.

There are also Generation ScotY contributors on most of the collective or aggregate blog sites. James Corbett produces articles regularly at *Think Scotland* while *Bella Caledonia* features a host of Generation ScotY contributors, including Dan Paris, Nine and James Maxwell. And then there is Mair Nor a Roch Wind, a blogging collective made up of entirely Generation ScotY activists, all of whom are pro-independence, some of whom are Labour party members and which appears to have succumbed to the age-old tradition on the left of fighting amongst themselves, having entered into a critical blog dialogue with members of Radical Independence.

There are also multi-media resources popping up all over the web. Jack Foster and Christopher Silver's film *What if Can't Do Became Can Do?*, which gently pokes fun at the idea of Scotland going it alone and succeeding through the medium of a know-it-all neighbour, has had nearly 40,000 views; Glasgow Skeptics, a Glasgow University debating forum, filmed the whole of its independence debate and posted it online; and Women for Independence produced a video encouraging more women to vote Yes, involving largely unknown women's voices, both old and young.

There are Generation ScotY-ers just picking up a camera, giving themselves a pseudonym or a title, taking the germ of an idea and seeing how it plays out. There's the video from Neil S satirising claims for the positive economic case for the Union simply by posting footage of rundown town centres, pawnshops and unkempt neighbourhood facilities, and an online news channel, *Scottish Times*, fronted by Generation Y-ers (including the rare sight of a young woman from a black and ethnic minority [BEM] background), posting their own generated news content on a range of independence themes. *Imagining Scotland* by Andrew Redmond Barr captures anonymous thoughts on what independence might mean for Scotland, and while aspirational and somewhat romantic in its approach, also applies strong production values. These might all be amateur filmmakers, but what they produce is far from homemade.

Songs have been written by Generation ScotY-ers, including 'State of the Union' by Scottish rapper Loki and 'Marriage Counselling' by rap collective Stanley Odd; plays have been and are being penned and staged, including the National Theatre of Scotland running the *Great Yes, No, Don't Know 5 Minute Theatre Show*, 'created by anyone for an audience of everyone', which has provided a platform for Generation ScotY dramatists to present their thoughts on the independence debate; wish trees have been populated and photo montages collated. Everywhere there is a flourishing of artistic content to sit cheek by jowl with the political aspects of the referendum, inspired by it, spurned by it and nearly all of it being nurtured into life by Generation ScotY:

> Possibly the most exciting aspect of the independence debate so far has been the extent to which it has reinvigorated popular democracy in our corner of the world. The town-hall meeting is back with a vengeance,

activists mobilise across the country on a daily basis, and workplaces and living rooms are abuzz with a debate which is well-informed, passionate and creative. We are debating the future of our country in a way that is heart-felt yet inclusive, idealistic yet sensible, and serious, yet with an ability not to take ourselves too seriously. This is what democracy looks like.

FRASER DICK, Generation Yes

Dear Britannia,
Things aren't right and we have to face it.
I don't appreciate the procrastination.
I'm just saying, it's not like you're pure amazing,
I'm fed up feeling like the poor relation.
And I don't appreciate yir passive aggression.
Is it too much to ask that you'd answer ma questions?
So I'm writing this metaphor, I've said it before.
I put more into us than you give me credit for.
We're needing some help. What makes you think I can't speak for myself?
And as for the division of wealth
I'm a 1,000-year-old country;
Surely, I'm old enough to look after my own money.
As for that nonsense about me being destitute,
Hen, I've got the same damn group of friends as you.
So stop implying that if you were to get shot of me
France, Germany and Spain wouldn't talk to me.
I feel like I'm banging ma head off a brick wall.
PS. Do you think of me at all?
Faithfully Yours,
Caledonia.

Dear Caledonia,
This grief is something that I wouldn't miss.
I'm tired of having to keep you in food and drink.
Since Culloden, it's been like a constant battle,
With you causing me nothing but hassle.
And you've been hellish short-tempered lately.
I thought we'd agreed to forgive and forget the '80s.
I've told you before how I actually felt.
I just don't think you can be trusted to look after yourself.

I know sometimes I don't give you enough attention,
But I've got a lot on ma plate with the current recession.
As for being mature enough to handle your financial payments?
Look at Greece, she's even older than you and they called in the bailiffs.
You show nothing but poor judgment. Why should I trust it?
Your tram fiasco? Way over budget.
Parliament building? Way over budget.
And you wonder why I don't want to discuss this?
Stop meddling, you're being childish and petulant.
And you wouldn't fare well in a divorce settlement.
Accept it. I know better. I don't need this added pressure.
PS. Weren't we always good together?
Sincerely Yours,
Britannia.

Britannia,
I don't appreciate yir tone. Wind yir neck in.
Don't even get me started on the years of oppression.
Every time I need money for spending
I shouldn't need to come begging for you to give it your blessin'.
I'm not a lap dog, a pet or a petulant wean.
I'm an equal and I expect to be treated that way.
I'm setting it straight. This is hardly blissful matrimony.
I've got resources so I shouldn't have to ask for money.
I support ma self so don't even mention alimony.
And I don't need you to fight ma battles for me.
So tell yir mates in Faslane they need a new address,
I see the truth with my new clear head.
Ma pal Alex says that you're blind to the facts
And that it's time for me to stand and draw a line in the sand.
Everybody's got an opinion and I'm sick of it.
I'm getting pulled in all directions with this constant bickering,
It's like a smokescreen I'm struggling to see through.
PS. Half of me doesn't want to leave you

Caledonia,
Bitch bitch moan moan. Give me a break,
All you ever seem to do is complain.

Maybe it's all that booze in your brain
Or you're woozy again from the smack running through your veins.
You're nothing but a drain on me and it's plain to see
You've developed more unhealthy habits that I need to pay to keep.
Basically you need stop your foolish ways,
Stop pulling away and start pulling your weight.

Pulling ma weight? Who do you think yir talking tae?
This is exactly what's making me want to walk away.
I'm tired of stating all ma reservations.
I think we should maybe try a trial separation.
You're blatantly economic with the facts.
Arrogant, self-centred, living in the past.
Reliving your former glory most days now,
Back when you were the biggest bully in the playground.
A shadow of your former self and it's plain to see.
You're falling apart and trying to put the blame on me.
I used to make things, inventions, you curbed my creativity.
You held me back, injured me by ending ma industry.
All I'm saying is the balance in the relationship isn't right.
Either change or I'm leaving, it's decision time.

Decisions? You don't have the power to make those
And you're not going anywhere unless I say so.
You're useless, who else would want you but me?
All the plans you make end in constant defeat.
You think we're really through?
All that's left of you is disease and booze. And you can't see the truth.
Obsessed with green and blue. After all we've been through,
I'd be doing you a favour keeping you.
Pipe down and stop being so mouthy.
The truth is you'd be nothing without me.
An alcoholic, sectarian, illiterate lout.
I'm providing the medicine and you're spitting it out.
Without me you won't last two minutes.
In fact I don't even care if we're finished.

David Hook (2012) with kind permission from Stanley Odd.

Generation ScotY mainstream activity

Alongside this explosion of activity around the referendum, mainstream youth movements are engaging Generation ScotY through information and in particular, voter registration activity. The Scottish Youth Parliament launched 'Aye, Naw, Mibbe' on National Voter Registration Day, with the aim of registering, engaging and informing Generation ScotY not just for the referendum, but the European and UK elections too in 2014 and 2015 respectively. As Kris Chapman, a Member of the Scottish Youth Parliament, says: 'Aye, Naw, Mibbe is a youth-led voter engagement project. Made by young people for young people.' It has a youth engagement team, will be undertaking outreach to communities and to young people through other organisations and has trained peer educators to carry out this work.

Kyle Thornton, Chair of the Scottish Youth Parliament, sets out the rationale behind Aye, Naw, Mibbe:

> The importance of ensuring the inclusion of young people in this debate cannot be emphasised enough. Through our work at the Scottish Youth Parliament we have found that young people are interested and want to influence the decisions that affect their future. We have also found young people can be put off by party politics. If they have access to sources of factual and robust information, and answers to the questions they are concerned about, then they are more likely to be engaged and therefore more likely to cast their vote.

Young Scot also has an interest in engaging Generation ScotY and provides information through web-based resources on the referendum, including a guide on six easy steps to voting, five reasons to vote and how to form a political opinion. None of it is fancy, but its straightforward, informative style – together with Young Scot being a 'brand' which young people up to the age of 25 engage with and trust – means it has an extensive reach to the Generation ScotY audience. Elsewhere, NUS Scotland is also encouraging students to register to vote on 18 September in the referendum. NUS Scotland has not taken a position on the referendum to support a Yes or No vote: instead, its focus is on getting students the information they need to decide how to vote.

The referendum is dominating the mainstream news agenda too, with scarcely a day going by without coverage attributable to both sides of the campaign in newspapers, on TV and radio, web and blog sites. While some might feel disengaged from it, there can be few in Generation ScotY who know absolutely nothing about it.

The referendum has also prompted a plethora of academic studies and research projects, but none of it has focused on Generation ScotY's attitudes towards this seminal vote. While there is plenty of data showing their voting intentions from polling (as we shall see), there has been little analysis of its meaning to date and there appears to have been no research undertaken to explore their views or opinions on independence, staying within the Union or indeed, other aspects relating to the debate. However, there is activity focussing on 16 and 17 year olds who will be participating for the first time in a vote in the UK. The BBC has set up a dedicated project called Generation 2014, with a panel of 50 16–17 year olds from across Scotland to take part in a range of activities in the run up to the vote, including a debate with representatives from the Yes and No campaigns, online thought pieces from some of the participants and engaging the group on key points and issues as they make up their minds how to vote.

Dr Jan Eichhorn of Edinburgh University has also been funded to investigate the attitudes of these young Scots, exploring their views on independence, national identity and political interests. His research is producing some interesting findings, not least that 16–17 year olds are less inclined to support Independence than 18–24 year olds, who are at the younger end of the Generation ScotY cohort (Eichhorn, 2013).

When trying to establish why this might be, Eichhorn considered issues of national identity, finding that more 16–17 year olds are less inclined to consider themselves solely Scottish than 18–24 year olds. The research report asserts that:

> Apparently one reason why young people are less likely to support independence is because they are more inclined to feel a dual sense of identity – a product perhaps of being the first generation to have grown up in a digitised world in which interpersonal communication is no longer bound by geography.
>
> EICHHORN, 2013

While this is true, surely it is also true of 18–24 year olds and indeed, all of the Generation ScotY cohort, who are considered just as much Digital Natives, and who are as much children of the digital age and less bound by geographic boundaries. As McCrindle suggests in exploring characteristics of Australian Generation Y, their influences are global musical artists, international events of significance and technological devices which are as available in Melbourne as Musselburgh or Mallaig (McCrindle, 2012). Some Generation ScotY members who are voting Yes have rejected the idea of independence as representing a choice based on identity or one which will lead to boundaries being erected between people living in Scotland and the rest of the UK: 'Because you probably need to take a long difficult look at yourself if you think that carrying a different passport from someone will be a barrier to your closeness.' (Kieran Hurley, one of his 25 reasons for voting Yes).

Moreover, other research has shown that while Generation ScotY has a stronger sense of being Scottish than young people under 18, their Scottish identity is less strong than that of older age groups. There is also evidence to suggest that in the last few years, their sense of having a multi-layered identity has grown, reducing the numbers who consider themselves solely to be Scottish (see Chapter 1). And for every 16 or 17 year old who can be found with a complex identity structure and a definite intention to vote No, then so can a 20-something be found with a similarly complex, multi-layered identity who is intending to vote Yes:

> My father comes from Mindanao in the Philippines and his father was from Madrid. My mother is from Manila. I was born and raised in Vancouver, Canada, and now live permanently in Scotland. I suppose that makes this the Spanish-Filipino-Scottish-Canadian take on the independence referendum, which I suspect is a fairly unusual one.
>
> THERESA MUNOZ

Generation Y and Z share too many common influences and a lack of boundaries for the shift in identity to be explicable by perceived digital status alone. Indeed, as one Better Together youth rep has stated: 'The world is changing, it's more connected than ever. I live here but my world goes beyond our border.'

Eichhorn also suggests that 16–17 year olds are more likely to vote No because they are more concerned about independence and its consequences than 18–24 year olds. Findings from Eichhorn's research, taken alongside the Scottish Social Attitudes Survey 2012, show that significantly more 16–17 year olds are 'quite' or 'very worried' about independence. Yet, other research shows that Generation Y in the UK is just as concerned about big policy ticket numbers like the economy and unemployment: indeed, Generation ScotY has felt the negative impact of the financial crisis and downturn more directly than their younger counterparts. Many voters of all ages are worried about the affordability of independence and whether Scotland can 'go it alone' economically. Why should those worries transfer into unease about independence itself for 16–17 year olds but less so for 18–24 year olds?

Neither of Eichhorn's explanations is wholly satisfactory. While the lack of geographic boundaries might enable more global influences, the converse is also true. The youngest generation of referendum voters has grown up more than any other with very British televisual and sporting influences, as well as international ones. There is virtually no Scottish oriented, Scottish produced TV or radio content targeted at the teen market. Specifically to address this deficit of content produced in Scotland, the BBC moved a prime time series, *Waterloo Road*, north of the border. We now have a drama series about life in a school being made in Scotland, with a sprinkling of Scottish accents added to the cast to assuage the natives, showcasing the English education system to a UK audience, apparently unaware that the system in Scotland is quite different, in terms of structure, governance and curricular content and approach. You couldn't make it up.

Children in Scotland are growing up influenced by what the BBC considers to be UK content but which is largely English in focus and nature. When was the last time that a literary classic from Scotland, Wales or indeed, Northern Ireland, was turned into a sumptuous period drama? Are there any CBBC programmes made in Scotland, with Scots, about life in Scotland? How many history series focusing on English kings and periods of solely English history, without making any reference to what was happening in Scotland at that time, have been made in recent years? How many 'Great British' spin-offs have been broadcast which are dominated by English regional accents? How many Scottish bands make it on to *Later with Jools Holland*?

It's not just the BBC. ITV's *Britain's Got Talent* didn't even bother to visit Scotland this year to see if we had any. There's *Made in Chelsea*, *Geordie Shore* and *The Only Way is Essex*: is there similar output showcasing the lives, loves, dramas and tantrums of young adults from Scotland? There's little Scottish football on terrestrial television at times when teenage Scots are likely to watch, and only Andy Murray can be heard regularly on the airwaves as one of our few contemporary world-class athletes.

On one level, this might not matter. Except that it does. If your entire childhood and adolescence has been spent watching and listening to non-Scots voices, non-Scottish towns, non-Scottish history, geography, culture, sport and interests, how can young people hope to have a sense of their Scottish identity? Add to that the fact that technology enables young adults in Scotland to access global media, to be as besotted with international artists and bands, sports stars and video games as their peers in other Western countries, so that they hear as many American accents as they do Scottish ones. What we have is a multi-layering, which creates a sort of hybrid identity that is not based in any physical sense in one place.

But it might not matter in terms of whether either generation chooses to vote No. There is little evidence to suggest that identity is a key reason for voting one way or the other; any link between 16–17 year olds feeling less Scottish and more British and their intention to vote No in greater numbers than those aged 18–24 is pure supposition. Indeed, if identity was a key factor, it might result in fewer bothering to vote or engage at all, yet all around, young adults of all ages are getting involved in the debate on Scotland's future at school, college, university and through organisations, movements and campaign groups, both mainstream and grassroots.

Why is Generation Scot Y fired by the debate on Independence?

If we can largely discount identity as a motivating factor for Generation Scot Y and that Scottish 20-somethings are just as likely to be concerned about the uncertainties surrounding independence as other voters, then we need to look elsewhere for factors influencing the level of their engagement with the referendum debate. What is firing their imaginations? Examine what they say themselves about why they support and oppose independence and vision appears foremost in their thoughts:

> I believe the politics of an Independent Scotland will reflect a fairer and more just society for all.
>
> Anonymous Imagine Scotland video participant

> I believe that in the years to come the challenges we will face will become global, requiring a larger united response. Being a part of the United Kingdom allows us to meet these challenges, as a voice on the world stage, with a

confidence and vigour knowing that our country is safe against even the strongest of threats to our future.

LACHLAN, Better Together Youth rep

The referendum on independence is all about the future and what kind of country Scotland might or could be. Indeed, both the official Yes and No campaigns have focused on notions of fairness, equality and social justice in framing their arguments: given that Generation ScotY is more likely to be attracted by such socially liberal concepts and also appears to have a sense of being community- and collectively-minded, the very defining characteristics of this generation demonstrate why engaging with the referendum might appeal.

Moreover, both campaigns are using multi-media and social media platforms to reach voters, methods which will appeal to Generation ScotY and crucially, will reach them. The campaigns are also participative and emotional and there is also space, particularly on the Yes side, for Generation ScotY to get involved by doing their own thing, to tell their stories. The very nature of the referendum – giving people a say in the future shape and direction of Scotland – will be empowering for some who for too long have felt outside politics. These are campaigns in which the main political parties in Scotland have a huge say, but not exclusively so: there is room for the voices of Generation ScotY to be heard and to feel that their voice is being heard.

In their own words – how Generation ScotY is articulating its views in the referendum debate

Members of Generation ScotY involved in both sides of the debate are using remarkably similar language to articulate why they support or oppose independence. Taking the words of a Better Together video targeted at young people and the words from young artists and creatives forming part of National Collective's 100 New Voices, these two word clouds demonstrate the phrases and words that each group use most often.

Take all the key phrases from Better Together's video message for young people and the words that resonate are: better, opportunities, future, together and choice. Take the key phrases from some of the 100 New Voices of the Independence Generation gathered by National Collective and some of

opportunities
together better
risk working
choose big best lives choice future
human rights question role linked break positive stronger strength solidarity worlds different makes strengths
security issues family strong jobs British interdependence campaigning increased proud stick worked great Scottish LGBT biggest saving decision away

make nation chance build equal people better country future
Scotland
society
democracy change best world ability democratic new
opportunity independence government progressive
decisions create need help rights
Westminster fairer want social system true values
generations energy powers words young challenges
compassionate forward welcoming culture
hatred caring generation just

the words that stand out are: better, opportunity, future, society and people. There's not a lot of difference in these main themes.

Research suggests that Generation Y is assertive, wants to be inspired, to be supported and appreciated, that its members have dominant social needs, are detached from traditional institutions, place high value on peer-to-peer activity and have high expectations (Taylor and Keeter, 2010). These characteristics provide clues to why they have responded so willingly to the referendum debate.

Their inspiration is derived from the possibilities and the opportunities presented by both a Yes and No vote – in obviously different ways. Listen to and read what they say and it is not about being led in an inspiring way to a 'better future,' but leading themselves there.

Generation ScotY campaigners are excited by equality issues – the Better Together word cloud highlights 'rights' in several places, while many of the 100 New Voice statements focus on what one sums up as the 'chance to move towards a more progressive, egalitarian society, which supports and celebrates the diversity of the many.' But they are also concerned with 'issues' as much as 'visions': across a wide range of public opinion surveys, the two issues influencing how Generation ScotY will vote are the economy and employment, though their options are clearly constrained by the pollsters providing a set list of issues to choose from.

These are not exclusive observations. They fit with what surveys suggest Generation Y in the UK is concerned with and which might, therefore, be encouraging 20-somethings in Scotland to engage with the referendum debate. The economy is one of the key battlegrounds in the referendum debate, particularly on the potential impact of independence on jobs. The big hitters in both campaigns appear to be on a speech a week in terms of spelling out their key messages and themes relating to what a YES or NO vote might mean. And so long as the campaigns keep trying to inspire, the more likely Generation ScotY is to engage and stay engaged. But engagement is not participation: how likely is Generation ScotY to turn out and vote on 18 September?

CHAPTER 5

The Future is Coming On

People of my generation have been called so many things – materialistic, hedonistic, obsessed with reality TV, maybe even a lost generation. Do you know what, that's just not true and I'm so fed up of hearing it. It's just that we've been without a voice for so long. Statistics now show that young people and low paid workers are more likely to be convinced of independence than any other group. Because we have everything to vote for. We have hope at last.

CAT BOYD, Generation Yes

It will affect not just us but the opportunities of future generations... We can have the best of both worlds, a Scottish Parliament with more powers and the opportunity of being part of one of the biggest economies in the world... We can do so much more when we work together. We want to stay together... for our future. So let's not leave. We're better together.

Generation ScotY participants in Better Together Youth video

Generation ScotY will have to live with the consequences of the vote in September for most of their adult lives. So the outcome of the referendum matters, to them as much if not more than others. You'd like to think that they are taking it seriously and giving it some thought. The quotes above offer assurance that they are: heartfelt, earnest, informed. Generation ScotY on both sides of the debate is engaged and involved and thinking hard about how to vote. So which side is winning the hearts, minds and, crucially, the votes of Generation ScotY? Indeed, do they intend to vote at all? The answer to the second question is yes and it would appear in greater numbers than for the 2016 Scottish Parliamentary elections:

Likelihood to vote in Independence referendum						
	YouGov	TNS BMRB	IPSOS Mori	YouGov	TNS BMRB	IPSOS Mori
	Feb-14	Feb-14	Mar-14	Feb-14	Feb-14	Mar-14
	18–24	16–24	16–24	25–39	25–34	25–34
Definite	65%	69%	56%	71%	76%	66%
Probably	6%	6%	11%	8%	9%	7%
Undecided	5%	4%	11%	5%	10%	4%

The likelihood of Generation ScotY to vote is still lower than older age groups but it is significantly higher than the intention to vote expressed in polls for 'ordinary elections,' which tends to hover below the 50 per cent mark. While there is some disagreement among pollsters, two out of three of the leading polling companies appear to show that most 20-somethings are certain or definite to vote. And the trend appears to be that the closer we get to referendum day, the more likely Generation ScotY is to turn out and vote.

What can be discerned from the polls about the voting intentions of Generation ScotY? Taking three of the leading polling companies in turn, the findings are quite different, depending on who is doing the polling. What must also be factored into the analysis is that the polling companies do not all use the same age definitions: for two of its three polls, ICM collated 25–44 year olds together, only changing tack and separating into two separate age groups in March this year.

The table below sets out the findings from three recent polls by IPSOS Mori, conducted at a year to go, at the turn of the year and at 200 days to go, until the referendum:

IPSOS Mori	Should Scotland be an independent country?			
16–24		Sep-13	Dec-13	Feb-14
	Yes	28%	29%	29%
	No	58%	57%	55%
	Undecided	14%	16%	16%
25–34				
	Yes	49%	52%	44%
	No	36%	28%	37%
	Undecided	16%	20%	19%

As suggested by other research (Eichhorn, 2013), IPSOS Mori shows a distinct difference in voting intentions between Generation ScotY at the younger end of the spectrum and those near the top. But these polls also show a high degree of variance in voting intentions over a relatively short period of time, particularly in the older age group. They also suggest that a significant minority has yet to make up its mind.

ICM's polls show a markedly different picture:

ICM	Should Scotland be an independent country?			
16–24		Sep-13	Jan-14	Mar-14
	Yes	18%	44%	30%
	No	59%	33%	42%
	Undecided	23%	23%	29%
25–34				
	Yes	32%	38%	44%
	No	43%	39%	41%
	Undecided	25%	23%	15%

This time, the variance is with the younger age cohort in Generation ScotY, with the older age group showing steady and marked gains for Yes. Yet more of both age groups are still undecided according to this pollster and overall, the voting intentions recorded are significantly different between the two polling companies across both age groups.

TNS BMRB has a longer range of polls to call on:

TNS-BMRB Scottish Opinion Monitor	Should Scotland be an independent country?					
16–24		Mar-13	Oct-13	Dec-13	Feb-14	Apr-14
	Yes	36%	18%	25%	29%	29%
	No	44%	43%	37%	40%	34%
	Undecided	20%	38%	38%	31%	37%
25–34						
	Yes	41%	26%	35%	24%	33%
	No	47%	34%	31%	36%	31%
	Undecided	12%	41%	34%	40%	37%

Again, there is variance, this time in both age ranges, though TNS BMRB's polls would suggest that from an early high point, support for Yes has tailed off somewhat. But then so has support for a No vote. Curiously, this pollster suggests that the closer we get to referendum day, so Generation ScotY becomes less sure how to vote. This differs from the findings of the other two polling companies.

Can trends be determined about the voting intentions of Generation ScotY in the independence referendum? Not really, as this graphic combining the poll results makes clear.

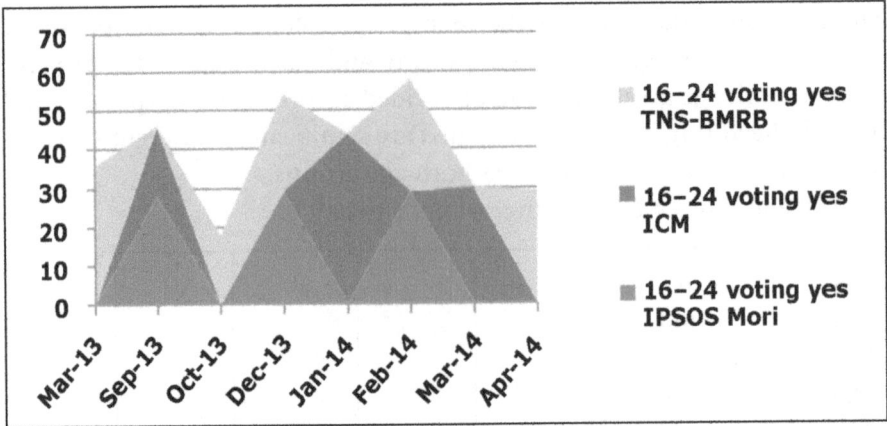

In the 16–24 age group, there is a marked difference across the three polling companies and also within the polls conducted by each. While ICM has support for a Yes vote softening and declining, TNS BMRB has it resurgent. IPSOS Mori is the only company to find some stability in levels of support for Yes, albeit at a significantly lower level than for No, which commands over 50 per cent support in this age group.

Similarly, it is difficult to see much in the way of a steady march of progress towards a Yes vote in the 25–34 age group. Indeed, all the pollsters seem to suggest that support for Yes might have peaked at the turn of the year but clearly, there is no real pattern, with gains and losses across all the polls which are quite marked.

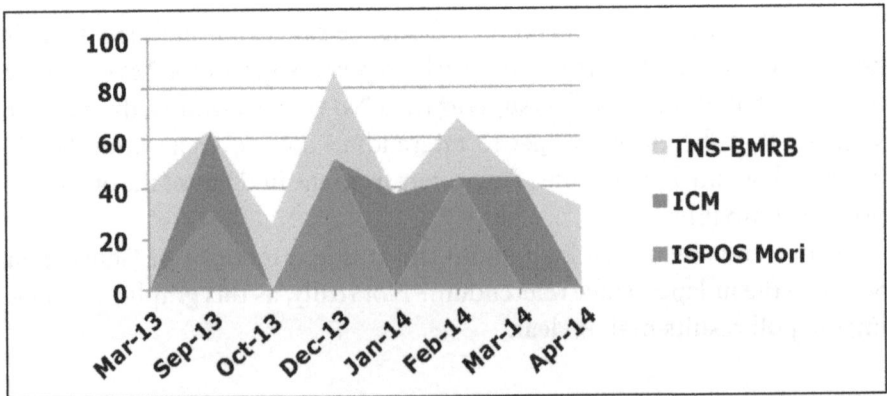

In fact, the only safe conclusion that can be drawn from this snapshot across three reputable polling companies is that the pollsters are all over the place with these age groups. There is little consistency and no evidence of a trend. This might be down to relatively small sample sizes in these omnibus surveys, or the use of different methodologies.

Any interpretation of the voting intentions of Generation ScotY is therefore highly tentative. It can be seen that more intend to vote in the referendum than tend to vote in elections. That can only be a good thing. A significant number of voters in these age groups have also to make up their minds how to vote – or at least, say how they have made up their minds. They are swinging back and forth, though it does appear that a sizeable majority of the younger cohort will be voting No. While those over 25 are showing a propensity to vote Yes, it would seem that their votes can yet be persuaded. While younger members of Generation ScotY appear to be firmly placed to vote No, on balance, it would appear that the older members favour Yes. But if both campaigns want to firm up support among Generation ScotY, they clearly have some work to do.

> Young people need to be given clear answers about the different options for their future, free from spin and polished answers. If young people have this information, a clear understanding of the options available to them and an opportunity to speak to the campaigns on their own terms, in their own environment, getting real answers to their questions, they will engage, they will think about their futures, they will vote.
>
> KYLE THORNTON, Chair, Scottish Youth Parliament

These surveys' findings are backed up by evidence elsewhere. Most of the universities, largely through student-led societies, have held Yes/No debates and polls. Of the five Scottish universities holding mock polls, all recorded No votes, with some significant margins of victory: at Aberdeen, No won by 64 per cent to 36 per cent; at Glasgow and also Glasgow Caledonian, No won by 63 per cent to 37 per cent; at Strathclyde, the margin was lower with No recording 55 per cent to Yes's 35 per cent; and at Dundee, it was 59 per cent to No, 41 per cent to Yes. (Better Together 2014)

What about those in Generation ScotY who are hardest to reach and easiest to ignore?

Work is under way to reach the Generation ScotY elements of Scotland's 'Missing Million' (Hassan, 2012): the million voters, largely from deprived communities, who are not registered to vote and have rarely, if ever, actually voted. To understand the scale of this, in one ward in Edinburgh South, the most deprived in the Parliamentary constituency, there are 800 households not registered on the electoral roll.

Because those supporting Independence and a Yes vote see it as in their favour to encourage more of the 'Missing Million' to register and participate, much of this activity is theirs. The Radical Independence Campaign is conducting mass canvass days and evenings in areas such as Dumbiedykes in Edinburgh and Drumchapel in Glasgow. Yes Scotland in Edinburgh holds Super Saturdays on the first Saturday of every month, visiting each of the Edinburgh Parliamentary constituencies, targeting the most deprived communities, with a focus on voter registration as much as on leafleting and canvassing. Women for Independence, a campaign group set up by women to reach out to female voters, is also focussing on women in Generation ScotY in deprived communities, many of whom will never have registered to vote nor voted before, despite some of them having had ten elections to participate in before now. There are even two long-time community activists, both of whom long ago eschewed formal political activity but want to make a contribution to the Yes campaign, who every Saturday make their way to Craigmillar in Edinburgh and simply knock on doors, explaining the importance of why the residents should participate in this referendum, encouraging them to register to vote. Again, they are focussed particularly on Generation ScotY.

All this informal activity sitting alongside official efforts conducted by electoral registration officers would appear to be making a difference. On Voter Registration Day in February 2014, the Electoral Commission confirmed that nearly 4.1 million voters in Scotland are now on the electoral roll, while National Records of Scotland (NRS) advised that 80 per cent of the newly enfranchised 16–17 year olds eligible to vote had registered.

The level of registration resulting from such efforts suggests that Scotland's 20-somethings are taking the referendum as seriously as other age groups. Indeed, it demonstrates that they understand the importance of participating in the referendum:

> Young people, above all other groups, have a massive stake in this important decision about Scotland's future. It's vitally important that whatever our view is, we make that view known by casting our vote.

> KYLE THORNTON, Chair, Scottish Youth Parliament

While NRS data suggests that this flourishing of activity has translated into higher voter registration, there are still worrying pockets of very small growth and even decline in those areas where Scotland's 'Missing Million' are likely to be present. Thus, while increases of over 2.5 per cent have been recorded in Aberdeen City, Aberdeenshire, City of Edinburgh, Midlothian, Moray and Stirling, increases of less than one per cent have been recorded in East Ayrshire, Glasgow City, North Ayrshire, North Lanarkshire and South Lanarkshire local authority areas. More worryingly still, significant declines in the numbers of voters registered have been recorded in Inverclyde (-4.74 per cent), Renfrewshire (-3.88 per cent) and smaller ones in Clackmannanshire (-0.83 per cent) and West Dunbartonshire (-0.32 per cent). All of these local authorities are known to have high indices of deprivation and poverty.

The NRS does not provide an age breakdown of voters registered, except for 16–17 year olds, but it seems likely that increased numbers of 20-somethings will have registered to vote in areas of growth in registration. But it also follows that in areas of marginal growth and actual decline in registrations, then fewer 20-somethings will have registered to vote. Those 20-somethings who form part of the 'Missing Million' might well still miss out on their chance to vote in the referendum.

What or who is influencing how Generation ScotY will vote in the referendum?

The variance recorded by polling companies in Generation ScotY's voting intentions is perplexing. What could be causing them to swing back and forth between Yes and No and also, become more undecided as the campaign goes on? All three companies recorded a lift for Yes to a greater or lesser degree in or around the turn of the year. This could be attributed partly to the publication of 'Scotland's Future,' the White Paper on Independence produced by the Scottish Government. It could also be a bit of a New Year resolution thing, with voters focusing their minds as the referendum campaign hits the final straight after a long two years of jousting. The decline in No support recorded by TNS-BMRB between February and April this year might be linked to the stushie over currency, when the UK Government ruled out an Independent Scotland entering into a currency union, as the Scottish Government had declared its preference for doing. It might also be down to Generation ScotY being less than impressed with Scottish Labour's Devolution Plus proposals. Or could David Bowie's intervention at the BRIT awards, through his proxy Kate Moss, pleading with Scotland to stay have caused some 16–24 year olds surveyed by ICM in March to switch from Yes to No? The fact is that there is no way of knowing, though it will be interesting to try and match up Generation ScotY voting intentions with big announcements and points of debate in the last few months of the campaign.

In Chapter Three, we saw how Generation ScotY is increasingly veering away from their parents' voting choices and habits for Scottish Parliament elections. Is there a similar lack of parental influence over voting intentions in the referendum?

	Yes			No			Undecided		
	Feb 14	Mar 14	Mar 14	Feb 14	Mar 14	Mar 14	Feb 14	Mar 14	Mar 14
16–24	29%	30%	29%	55%	42%	34%	16%	29%	37%
25–34	44%	44%	33%	37%	41%	31%	19%	15%	37%
35–54	28%			56%			16%		
35–44		38%	26%		46%	33%		16%	41%
45–54		40%	41%		43%	39%		17%	20%

The February 2014 data is from IPSOS Mori's Scottish Opinion Monitor, the first set of March 2014 figures is from ICM's poll for *Scotland on Sunday* and the second set is from TNS BMRB. Clearly, comparison across polls would be easier if the market research companies could agree age definitions. And if nothing else, this comparative analysis shows that the pollsters differ significantly on more than one age group, on both Yes and No intentions, as well as undecideds.

If there is one trend across all age groups, it is that the closer we get to the referendum, the less certain everyone becomes about how they intend to vote. Which is somewhat ironic, given that people have been asking consistently for 'more information' to help them make up their minds, yet the more they receive, the less certain they become. Generally speaking, we can see that by a significant margin, younger Generation ScotY voters are inclined to vote No; intention is more evenly divided between Yes and No among the older 20-somethings; voters aged 35-54 are more likely to vote No than Yes; at the older end of this cohort, voting intention is more even.

Look across the generations and intentions become more symmetrical. The voting intention between 16–24 year olds and 35–54 year olds is similar, as is the case between 25–34 year olds and those aged 45–54. What this seems to suggest is that Generation ScotY is more likely to be influenced by their parents' voting intentions in the referendum. This, of course, is quite different from intentions for the next Scottish Parliamentary elections. But there are also pockets of dissent.

Looking solely at the February 2014 data from IPSOS Mori (which also provided the data for the voting intentions' analysis in Chapter Three), it would appear that there are generational differences in voting intentions. Those aged 16–24 might be more inclined to follow their parents' lead (voters aged 35–54) with almost identical voting intentions but those aged 25–34 seem determined to vote differently. Many more of them are more inclined to vote Yes than older voters. The same is true among those intending to vote No.

Rather than the somewhat bold intentions to vote differently from their parents, Generation ScotY appears remarkably conformist in its referendum voting intentions. Far from being radical and opting in significant numbers for a Yes vote, certainly in the youngest age group, there is a suggestion of a conservative, safety-first attitude. It's a far cry from being feted as the Independence Generation, so what might be driving it?

Different but the same

It is not clear what influence identity has on referendum voting intentions among Generation ScotY. The two sources' findings on self-perceptions of identity are the 2011 Census and the State of the Nation survey for British Future. Both seem to contradict the findings used by Eichhorn to claim that identity is playing a role in determining how 16–17 year olds might vote.

Because of the different age definitions used – can we get a law to insist upon the same ones being used by all data sources? – Caution must be applied. But looking solely at those under 24, there would appear to be no correlation between identity and referendum voting intention: voters aged 16–24 are most inclined to vote No, yet 60 per cent of those aged 20–24 consider themselves 'solely Scottish' in identity (Census, 2011). Yet, this does not hold true for older Generation ScotY members: voters aged

25–34 are most likely to be intending to vote Yes and 58 per cent of adults aged 25–29 consider themselves 'solely Scottish' (Census, 2011). For one age cohort there would appear to be a link, but not for another.

Eichhorn suggested that growing up in a globalised society, in a world without boundaries or borders, might be influencing young people to vote No. Yet, Generation ScotY activists both cite internationalist reasons for their position:

> In an increasingly globalised world, the internet, culture and social media increasingly blurs traditional boundaries. Young people are at the forefront of this by sharing ideas and a culture that is bigger than parochial nationalism.
>
> ANYA O'SHEA, Better Together Youth rep

> Independence is… Progressing as a peaceful, culturally diverse nation, striving for healthier and fairer links with our neighbours, whilst speaking with its own voice internationally.
>
> CALUM STEWART, #TradYes musician

> I would rather Scotland had a significantly smaller voice in the international community so long as it is one of compassion and dignity.
>
> MIRIAM BRETT, Women for Independence and Generation Yes

Moreover, both cite the UK as either opportunity or barrier to achieving their aspirations as global citizens:

> Young people realise the blindingly obvious fact that the institutions which shape their lives and fuel their future are very often British institutions. Alex Salmond is wrong and out of touch to think that we want to split apart from our friends across the border. Alex Salmond is wrong because he doesn't treat the UK as a family.
>
> ANYA O'SHEA, Better Together Youth rep

> I sense how different Scotland is from Westminster already and as a young, global citizen committed to living and working in Scotland, I don't feel represented by the UK Government's increasingly inward-looking, predominantly male, predominantly white, culture.
>
> THERESA MUNOZ, National Collective

Indeed, so significant does Better Together consider these issues for young voters, that Alistair Darling, putative head of the No campaign, devoted an entire speech to the theme of 'No borders between our young people and opportunity'.

While identity and sense of self and place are clearly playing a role in determining Generation ScotY's attitudes to the referendum and how they intend to vote, it is not the critical factor. These issues are influencing young adults' decisions on both sides of the argument. What seems more important to those who are showing a greater propensity to vote no, appears to be the idea of living in a world without borders, in a Scotland which remains part of a bigger entity in the UK. Yet, this is viewed by many of those inclined to vote yes as a constraint, with being part of the UK preventing Scotland from serving a more fulfilling, international role, as a player on the world stage. So if not identity, then what?

Safety in numbers

We have seen in previous chapters how Generation ScotY has been hardest hit by the harsh economic situation in terms of unemployment, inequality and income. Research has suggested that these issues are of significance to this age group. Could these weighty political matters be nudging them to vote No?

Throughout the debate, commentators have tried to get into the minds of voters to work out what is driving them to vote Yes or No. The perceived wisdom, through skilful messaging and positioning largely by Yes Scotland and the Scottish Government, is that those urging Scotland to vote No are driven by negativity and are trying to scare the Scots into staying put. This is in stark contrast – so the narrative goes – to the offer of independence, which is about opportunity and aspiration. Voting Yes represents a positive choice, voting No a negative one. Take that to its conclusion and younger voters should surely be opting for Yes in their droves. Beset by unemployment with their life chances threatened as a result, earning less than their parents and likely to remain so throughout their adult lives, if ever an age group needed a negative environment from within which to reject the constitutional status quo, surely it is this one? Yet, this is the age group most likely to vote No.

So, clearly the issues of unemployment and economy, far from herding Generation ScotY to Yes (certainly at the younger end of its spectrum) appear to be propelling them to No. However, it may well be that the older Generation ScotY members – those hurtling towards their 30s and who have jobs, families of their own and increasing responsibilities – do see a link between voting Yes and the current economic situation.

Read any of Yes-supporting Generation ScotY's testimony – National Collective's 100 New Voices of the Independence Generation is a good place to start – and few cite better job prospects or a wealthier economy as the main impetus for their decision to vote for independence. Graeme Sneddon is the exception rather than the rule:

> I support independence because it provides the best opportunity to tackle the major problems facing Scotland. Only with the economic powers of an independent Scottish Parliament can we tackle youth unemployment head on and protect the most vulnerable in society, with firm investment in key industries and education and making our own compassionate welfare state.

While both campaigns have made a pitch for young voters using the economic arguments, it would appear that Better Together's efforts have resonated more with Generation ScotY, particularly the under 24s. It appears to have tapped more effectively into the fears and concerns of young people, as evidenced in the recent Carrington Dean 'teen money survey' among 1,000 15–17 year olds in Scotland, which found that 64 per cent of 15–17 year olds worry about the economic outlook in independent Scotland and 39 per cent think their own generation would be financially worse off in an Independent Scotland with only a quarter thinking they would be better off (Carrington Dean, 2014).

Even though the offer through independence is significant – more civil service jobs based in Scotland, continued free university tuition, signing up to the European Youth Guarantee, raising the minimum wage, encouraging a living wage – it is also unquantified:

> A Yes vote means that we will have the economic powers we need here in Scotland to grow the economy and create jobs. That means more opportunities for young people to work and build a career in Scotland.
>
> Yes Scotland, 2014

It is left to voters to work out the what, the how and the how many and it would seem that is not enough to entice more of Generation ScotY to vote Yes. There is an element – liberally articulated in Better Together's messaging – that Generation ScotY would be better off with the 'devil it knows,' or as they put it, 'the best of both worlds.' It appears to be working.

Hands up who wants a fairer, more just Scotland

At the heart of the campaign for independence is a key premise: if we want to create a fairer, more just Scotland, we have to vote Yes and become Independent. To illustrate why, again the negatives of the current political and constitutional set-up are emphasised. We get governments we didn't vote for. Worse, we get Tory governments we didn't vote for. The bedroom tax as an example of an unfair and unjust policy has become a *cause celebre*. Women have been highlighted as being hard done by. Even farmers are getting a raw deal under the current UK Government.

There has been a smattering, too, of the sort of policies we could look forward to which help to create a fairer and more just Scotland, particularly on childcare and taxation. Given Generation ScotY's inclination to be more socially liberal, it would seem to be a winning formula. These lofty ideals certainly seem to have fired up many of the Yes-supporting Generation ScotY luminaries. When asked why they are voting for independence, many cite the desire for far-reaching change – a shift in culture, the chance to create a fairer, more equal society:

> It's not simply about economics, the SNP or Tories, but the chance to change course – to take stock and reassess what we're doing. Independence is the beginning of a fantastic journey, a wonderful opportunity where we get the chance to create a better country. One that's fit for the modern world and which can adapt quickly to modern challenges. A country that views everyone as equal, treats them fairly and wants to look after itself a wee bit, stay fit and healthy.
>
> DAVID OFFICER, National Collective

As much as these are positive reasons to vote Yes, they are also predicated on a negative: the situation is so dire and so unlikely to improve under the current system that we need to move on to something new and start again. David Officer explains:

> So, look at the country around you... take a good long look. Britain is shit. We're stuck in this self-destructive merry-go-round of public school suits who only experience Scotland when shooting deer on the bare, barren hills, that have been dredged of all other life, lest it spoil their authentic highland experience. But we can move forward and show what can be done with a bit of will and the chance to have our say. It can be transformational, not just for Scotland, but for the whole of the UK, by

letting our voices soar above the bawling, braying bunch of naysayers and doom merchants and having a wee bit of faith in ourselves; a wee bit of hope.

Generation ScotY members who intend to vote No also express a commitment to the ideals of fairness through the sense of belonging to a UK family. One even appropriates Robert Burns to make his case: 'Robert Burns realised that when we in this island are united, we are able to meet and overcome challenges due to our collective strength. This is a belief I share' – (Jamie, Better Together Youth.)

If both Yes and No supporting Generation ScotY members share a belief in their position representing opportunities for fairness and equality, what divides them is the outlook. No supporters focus on what we have now, with the status quo and life in the present as having been developed through a shared past. Yes supporters are more likely to be looking ahead, to the future and what independence might deliver.

The polls suggest that neither side has made a breakthrough with this key target group. Its voting intentions have swung this way and that and are still clearly up for grabs. And unlike voting intentions for the 2016 Scottish Parliamentary elections, Generation ScotY might well mirror their parents' voting intentions in the referendum. It is also difficult to correlate influencing factors, despite the best efforts of commentators and academics to ascribe a rationale for Generation ScotY's voting intentions. Even issues considered as important, if not intrinsic, to the independence debate, such as identity, appear not to have a causal link to 20-somethings' voting choice. The same is true for those issues that Generation ScotY considers important, such as employment, the economy and social policy issues like equality. Those advocating a No vote appear to have made a better fist of reaching out to the Generation ScotY audience, but it is marginal. To coin a phrase, Generation ScotY is a riddle wrapped in a mystery inside an enigma. And that makes them fascinating.

As one of the big groups of undecided voters left in the referendum campaign, the longer they adhere to this status, the more important they become to the outcome. But securing their votes might require the Yes and No movements to do and say things a little differently: their arguments and messaging are clearly not chiming. It might be tempting to discard Generation ScotY, given the relatively high numbers unlikely to vote, based on their past performance in elections, at least. But the older part of this demographic in particular, those over 25, does tend to vote. Polling suggests it is more inclined to vote yes and if Yes Scotland continues to aspire to a vision of a fairer Scotland and articulate the economic case for independence in ways that this age group of voters can understand and identify with, it may well clean up. Generation ScotY could yet become the Independence Generation and even the generation who delivered independence.

A Serious Generation for Serious Times

This is our time, our time of reckoning. We have to take it. And if we don't take it, we are consigning our children to much, much less. Certainly narrower horizons, lower aspirations. Consigning our children to being small when we should be giving them a much bigger world.

THE LATE MARGO MacDONALD MSP

SETTING OUT ON this journey to explore the political views and behaviours of Generation ScotY prompted a little introspection and reflection on my own experience of life in Scotland through my 20s. It was instructive, not least in realising that you really do experience an awful lot of growing up in that decade. But it was also good to recall that while my political views and allegiances had largely been formed in my teens, it was in my 20s that I became much more politically active. Why? Because I had a son and I wanted him to have a better life, a better Scotland to grow up in.

Trying to create a picture of life for this generation of 20-somethings was tough. Scotland gathers a lot of data; it just forgets to put it in one easy-to-find place. For a nation renowned for nosiness, we are remarkably uncurious about who we are and what makes us. It became clear that we lack a tradition in sociological demography, in using what we know about different generations – and the ones on the way up in particular – to evidence our policy development. Thus, to try to define Generation ScotY requires broad brushstrokes and a reliance on the swathe of studies conducted elsewhere in the Western world.

The US and Australia are almost obsessed with knowing more about and understanding Generation Y or Millennials, as they are also known. People have got rich on trying to explain who they are, how they think and what they do. This Generation matters because of its importance. It is the first working age population to have grown, not shrunk in size. This will be the generation expected to keep a huge retired and about-to-retire population of Baby Boomers and Generation Xers in the style to which they have become accustomed. Societies therefore need to ensure that their corner of Generation Y is equipped to earn, to work hard and long and to contribute to the communal pot, if economies are not to collapse under the burden and demand for care from burgeoning pensioner populations. You can almost sense the exasperation at the discovery that Generation Y employees are not prepared to settle for their lot, that they want a better working life than their parents, they want and expect to be respected, kept interested and to have a life beyond work (Donovan and Finn, 2013).

Consequently, some have dismissed Generation Y as essentially selfish and whiny: the generation that wants it all and wants it now. As a parent of a Generation ScotY, it's easy to buy into this depiction. Yet it is fundamentally not true. The fact that we in Scotland ignore ours, refusing to study their wants, needs, interests and desires in any great depth suggests the selfishness is all ours. Theirs is, after all, the generation paying for the error of our profligate ways, social, political and economic.

Generation ScotY might want it all, but it is Generation ScotX and the Baby McBoomers who have had it all. The legacy of massive government and personal debt, of a democracy staggering under the weight of its own indifference and greed, of institutions which have forgotten their purpose and of limited opportunities and aspirations is a poor one indeed. The only thing we have left behind for Generation ScotY is a morass that its members are going to have to spend their lifetimes sorting. Now, research suggests that Generation Y in the UK will be the first to earn less than their parents, to end up with narrower horizons. As Margo MacDonald put it in her last ever interview, we are consigning our children to small. Hands up if you're proud of that.

Whether it is cause or effect, as a society, we do little to ease the transition from childhood to adulthood. Indeed, our track record in Scotland in terms of investing in Generation ScotY to enable them to reach adulthood as confident and competent citizens is patchy. Curriculum for Excellence, with its focus on creating rounded rather than rote-retaining individuals, has come too late for this generation. Education maintenance allowances (EMAS) meant more of them got to stay on at school, especially among poorer households, and free university tuition means higher education has become more affordable for all. But we have failed since the dawn of devolution to close the attainment gap, meaning 20-somethings (and their younger counterparts) from 'scheme schools' will not have achieved the necessary qualifications which enable them to benefit from this policy.

One of the key characteristics of Generation ScotY is how they learn and who they learn from. Theirs is the first multi-modal generation who learn through experience and from their peers. They like the power of the story, an emotional hook and to participate (McCrindle, 2012). How many universities, colleges and indeed, workplaces encourage these methods? Even now, we refuse to shift our learning culture to include them, preferring instead to focus on producer interests. In an age of mass information, we generate little content which appeals to them: BBC Three has bitten the dust and in Scotland, there is not a single programme produced which caters for their tastes and interests. Indeed, we keep all things Scottish that might be of interest to them hidden from view.

Generation X stubbornly maintains the old ways, adapting digitally only when needs must. Our key institutional architecture and frameworks are constituted in ways that exclude Generation ScotY's participation. We neither enable nor encourage them, then have the temerity to excoriate them for their disinterest and disenfranchisement. Many have shrugged their shoulders and walked away, forming their own peer networks of support, which occasionally erupt in violence, such as during the riots in England in summer 2012 or the Arab Spring, which flared across the Middle East and North Africa between 2010 and 2013. But just as many seek to be included and knock politely at the door of established Scotland seeking entry.

And therein lies hope. For all our attempts to ignore and rebuff, Generation ScotY is remarkably resilient. This book barely scratches the surface of who and what constitutes Generation ScotY. Yet, the little that has been documented here is fascinating, particularly in how, with little support from their supposed elders and betters, Generation ScotY is making the most of their opportunities and determining to find their own way. If we thought we could mould them to fit our world view, then we might want to think again.

There are three exciting discoveries worth highlighting. First, Generation ScotY is less concerned with fripperies than we might imagine and certainly, than they are portrayed. They worry about big issues and again, that is the legacy we have bequeathed to them. The UK being the fourth most unequal society in the world has become a bit of a slogan and soundbite during the referendum debate. It trips off the tongues of Yes supporters readily, but how often do they – or anyone else – pause to consider what that actually means for Generation ScotY? Their adulthoods will be dominated with concern about debt and earning potential. They know that better than we do: it's one reason why they're so angry with their parents. But we can take heart from the fact that they take it all so seriously: it means that they also have a chance of finding a way out of the mess of older generations making.

Second, despite our best efforts to dissipate their optimism by raining on their parade, this is also a sunshine generation, forever looking on the bright side. Generation ScotY is determined to have more than the traditional Scottish 'half of a loaf' and that is a good starting point for adult life. Some of that is, of course, the predilection of youth: no mountain is so big that it cannot be climbed when you're 21 and have your life before you. The suggestion of a divide in optimism and expectation between the haves and have-nots (Princes' Trust, 2011) is concerning: if ways are not found to bridge the inequality gap, to stem the generational inequality developing as a result of this recession, then more of Generation ScotY will be ground down. The State, currently controlled by Generation X and the Baby Boomers, can and must do more. Acceptance of their lot could just as easily turn to civil disobedience and worse.

Much of this optimism has translated into engagement with the referendum debate enthralling Scotland. Generation ScotY is involved, interested and enthused. I've been campaigning in what is known as 'areas of multiple deprivation' in different parts of Scotland for three decades now. It has been nigh on impossible to persuade women in their 20s that voting is worth it: politics has always seemed like a far away business, divorced from the reality of their lives. Yet they – even they, especially they – are interested in what September is all about. I have watched several register to vote for the very first time: that in itself counts as a small triumph.

The fact that Generation ScotY is largely organising itself – the experiential peer thing – to participate in Scotland's great debate on its future is just as encouraging. They are finding ways to engage, with their own groups and movements springing up, as well as getting involved and informed through more mainstream activity, which is still largely by and for their generation. They now have myriad routes into participation and only good will come of that in the long term. Indeed, the fact that the efforts by the official Better Together and Yes Scotland campaigns appear rather threadbare is also a good thing, for it suggests that they are neither needed nor wanted.

Also heartening is that even though Yes and No Generation ScotY protagonists find themselves either side of a dividing line, their language, their focus and their narrative is broadly similar. Both are advocating their vision for Scotland's future in largely positive tones. They are motivated by hope, by a sense of community, by opportunity and by the chance for change. Generation ScotY on both sides see beyond traditional borders – they are after all a much more inter-connected generation – and it is hoped that they find ways to keep that going beyond the referendum in September and indeed, are enabled to keep that going. Where currently there is difference, if they can find ways to align their commonalities, then we may see a very different politics emerge in the aftermath of the referendum vote. At heart, Generation ScotY wants 'better.' We might want to heed that message. Moreover, those fearful that the current political polarisation will result in permanent rift might wish to ensure that Generation Scot Y is included in efforts at rapprochement and reconciliation. Whisper it, Generation ScotY could even be ideal to lead such activity.

The third discovery is that this is a resourceful generation capable of making decisions all on its own. Not so different from Generation X or even the Baby Boomers after all. Generation ScotY seems set to vote quite differently from Generation Y in the Scottish Parliamentary elections in 2016. And even while the polls suggest the generations might vote the same way in the referendum, there are still too many undecideds to be certain that the generations might not divide along the Yes and No lines. The traditional political parties, particularly Scottish Labour, might wish to mine this for their own narrow purposes (and there are worrying signs that this is exactly what Scottish Labour is doing, with only one eye on the independence referendum and the other fixed beadily on the 2016 Scottish elections). More of Generation ScotY than ever before is intending to vote in September: they have a stake in determining Scotland's and their future and they intend to claim it. But just like older generations, they have yet to be convinced which path to take. The polls suggest a conundrum: the closer we get to September, the more undecided they become.

It is far from certain that this is the Independence Generation and if they do become so, then it is not even clear that this will be of their own choosing. And there could be trouble ahead if Generation ScotY feels resentful of older generations if they bequeath them a future they neither wanted nor voted for. Indeed, if as some polls suggest, the older cohort in Generation ScotY (those aged 25–34) votes Yes to independence and the outcome is a No vote, then that result will most likely have been achieved through the votes of those over 45 and particularly, those aged over 60. In other words, Generation ScotY could be denied the future they want by the votes of their parents and grandparents. Such a situation might foment societal discord, particularly given the outlook for Generation ScotY in terms of their incomes and economic wellbeing. For all that it is a good thing that Generation ScotY is making its own mind up whether to vote Yes or No, their parents and grandparents might want to listen to their views before making up theirs.

This is a generation which is relaxed about who it is and where it belongs; Generation ScotY is comfortable with its multi-layered identities:

> I'm not a nationalist. I wouldn't even say I'm particularly patriotic. I would call myself a Shetlander first, and Scottish second. I probably wouldn't always have though. Growing up in Shetland, the idea of being 'Scottish' wasn't something I ever thought about.
>
> LOUISE THOMASON, National Collective

> I thought in a way that I'm a child of the Union. I'm Scottish, my dad's English, we're all British. What's the point of breaking up the UK? The point is we have a shared history, culture and experience with our friends and family all over the UK.
>
> HANNAH, Better Together youth rep

If identity is playing any part in shaping Generation ScotY's voting intentions in the referendum, it appears more of an influence on those who want to stay within the UK rather than those intending to vote Yes. Asserting their Scottishness does not appear to be high on their priorities. And while the economy and employment are issues that vex them, it is not clear if either of these policies are influencing Generation ScotY or even that the Yes and No campaigns have anything enticing to offer. Generation Y's proclivity for socially liberal policy matters appears to be shared by Generation ScotY, as evidenced by the remarkable response in favour of equal marriage. The language being used by Yes and No supporting Generation

ScotY members suggests that aspiration, vision and grand principles and notions of equality, fairness and opportunity are influencing them. The only problem for the campaigns is that these ideals motivate and resonate with supporters on both sides.

What has struck me throughout this mazy, hazy journey into the world of Generation ScotY is just how articulate it is. Their views on independence and on other political matters are considered, well thought out and constructive, and if they do help Scotland become Independent, then our future is in safe hands. Generation ScotY has not had an easy transition from childhood and those difficulties are likely to remain well into their middle age. Far from being the generation that wants it all, Generation ScotY wants but a little of all that we have had. And who can blame them for that? Ultimately, this is a serious generation for serious times. It's time older generations started taking and treating them as seriously as they deserve.

References

Ballard, M; Chapman, M., *et al.*, *Bright Green*, available at http://brightgreenscotland.org/. Last accessed 14.04.14.

Barr, A. R., (2013) *Imagining Scotland*. available at https://www.youtube.com/watch?v=3hghB-XZq38. Last accessed 05.05.14.

BBC Scotland (2014), *Generation 2014*, available at http://www.bbc.co.uk/news/uk-scotland-scotland-politics-26634609. Last accessed 02.05.14.

Bennet, E., *The Science of Independence*, available at http://scienceofindependence.wordpress.com/. Last accessed 14.04.14.

Better Together Youth. (2012), *Why we are Better Together*, available at https://www.youtube.com/watch?v=RxbAu3LphYM. Last accessed 04.04.14.

Brand, R. (2013), *Interview on BBC Newsnight by Jeremy Paxman*, BBC Newsnight, available at http://www.youtube.com/watch?v=3YR4CseY9pk. Last accessed 18.05.14.

Brett, M., (2014), *Independence is for me about three things*, Aye Talks, (unpublished observations).

Bromley, C., Curtice, J., Seyd B., (2004), *Is Britain facing a Crisis of Democracy?*, The Constitution Unit, UCL, available at http://www.ucl.ac.uk/spp/publications/unit-publications/112.pdf. Last accessed 18.05.14.

Bunzl, J., (2013), *Russell Brand: New Revolutionary?* Huffington Post, available at http://www.huffingtonpost.co.uk/john-bunzl/russell-brand-new-revolutionary_b_4170644.html. Last accessed 18.05.14.

Carrington Dean, (2014), *Scottish Teen Money Survey*, available at http://www.carringtondean.com/media/resources/STMS-PR.pdf. Last accessed 20.05.14.

Corbett, J., *Think Scotland*, available at http://www.thinkscotland.org/search.html?read_full=11936&article=www.thinkscotland.org. Last accessed 14.04.14.

Crain, R., (1993), *Generation Y*, No longer available at: http://adage.com/

Cribb, J., Hood, A., Joyce, R., Phillips, D., (2013) *Living Standards, Poverty and Inequality in the UK: 2013*, London: Institute of Fiscal Studies. p. 98, Figure 5.8; p. 100

Darling, A., (2014) *No Borders between our young people and opportunity*, Better Together, available at http://bettertogether.net/blog/entry/no-borders-between-our-young-people-and-opportunity. Last accessed 14.05.14

Donovan A., Finn D., (2013), *PwC's NextGen: a global generational study 2013*, available: http://www.pwc.com/en_GX/gx/hr-management-services/pdf/pwc-nextgen-study-2013.pdf. Last accessed 04.01.14.

Electoral Commission (2014), *Electoral Commission statement on publication of Scotland's Electoral Registers*, available at http://www.electoralcommission.org.uk/i-am-a/journalist/electoral-commission-media-centre/news-releases-referendums/electoral-commission-statement-on-publication-of-scotlands-electoral-registers. Last accessed 02.05.14.

Eichhorn, J., (2013), *Comparisons between the newly enfranchised voters and the adult population*, available at http://www.scotcen.org.uk/media/205540/131129_will-16-and-17-years-olds-make-a-difference.pdf. Last accessed at 08.04.14.

English-Kershaw, S., (2014), *Young People really are interested in politics*, Catch 21, available at http://www.catch21.co.uk/2014/02/young-people-interested-politics. Last accessed 18.05.14.

Foster, J., Silver, C., (2014), *What if can't do became can do?*, available at http://www.youtube.com/watch?v=dHW-RDJOJTo. Last accessed 13.04.14.

Gallacher, C., Scothorne, R., Westwell, A., *Mair nor a roch wind*, available at http://mairnorarochwind.wordpress.com/. Last accessed 14.04.14.

Glasgow Skeptics Society, (2014), *Should Scotland be an independent country?*, available at https://www.youtube.com/watch?v=UafGNaOEMNU. Last accessed 05.05.14.

Hannah (2014), *We have a shared history, culture and experience*. Better Together, available at http://bettertogether.net/blog/entry/better-together-youth-rep-hannah-we-have-a-shared-history-culture-and-exper. Last accessed 18.05.14.

Hassan, G. (2012), *The Missing Million Scots: What do you do when democracy fails you,* available at: http://www.gerryhassan.com/ uncategorized/the-missing-million-scots-what-do-you-do-when-democracy-fails-you/ Last accessed 30.04.14.

Henn, M., Foard, N., (2011) *Young people, political participation and trust in Britain,* ESRC and Nottingham Trent University, available at http://www.exeter.ac.uk/media/universityofexeter/research/ microsites/epop/papers/Henn_and_Foard_-_Young_People,_Political_ Participation_and_Trust_in_Britain.pdf Last accessed 08.04.14.

Holmes, T., (2013) *Demonising Russell Brand,* New Left Project, available at http://www.newleftproject.org/index.php/site/blog_ comments/demonising_russell_brand. Last accessed 18.05.14.

Horovitz, B., (2012), *After Gen X, Millennials, what should next generation be?,* available at http://usatoday30.usatoday.com/money/ advertising/story/2012-05-03/naming-the-next-generation/ 54737518/1?loc=interstitialskip. Last accessed 04.01.14.

Howe, N., Strauss, W., (2000), *Millenials Rising: the next Great Generation,* 3rd ed. USA: Vintage Books

Howker, E., Malik, S., (2010) (updated and revised 2013) *Jilted Generation: How Britain has bankrupted its youth,* Icon Books.

Hurley, K. (2014) *25 Reasons for Voting Yes,* National Collective, available at http://nationalcollective.com/2014/04/23/kieran-hurley-25-reasons-im-voting-yes/. Last accessed 18.05.14.

ICM (2013) *Scottish Independence,* available at (Sept 2013) http://www. icmresearch.com/data/media/pdf/2013_sept_scotland_independ-ence_poll1.pdf. Last accessed 18.05.14.

IPSOS Mori, (2014) *Global Trends Survey,* available at http://www. ipsos-mori.com/researchpublications/researcharchive/3369/People-in-western-countries-pessimistic-about-future-for-young-people. aspx. Last accessed 04.04.14.

IPSOS Mori, (2014) *Scottish Public Attitudes and Opinion Monitor – Wave 18,* available at (Feb 2014) http://www.ipsos-mori.com/ Assets/Docs/Scotland/ipsos-mori-scotland-monitor-tables-february-2014.pdf. Last accessed 14.04.14.

LGBT Youth Scotland M.E.2 campaign – youtube channel http://www. youtube.com/watch?v=WOxL-PuZW-4&list=PLC30D-B9A3937CD295

Loki (2014), *State of the Union,* available at https://www.youtube.com/watch?v=9QvYyvRn5HY. Last accessed 05.05.14.

McCrindle, M., (2012) *Generations Defined Sociologically*, available at http://mccrindle.com.au/resources/Generations-Defined-Sociologically.pdf. Last accessed 14.05.14.

McCrindle, M., (date unknown) *Understanding Generation Y)*, The Australian Leadership Foundation, pp. 1–6, available at http://www.rowingvictoria.asn.au/documents/gorowing/UnderstandingGenY.pdf. Last accessed 30.04.14.

McLean, B., (2014) *Releasing the Potential of Scotland's Young People*, Young Scot, available at https://storify.com/Lee_90K/young-scot-joint-event-with-solace-releasi. Last accessed 04.04.14.

Morrison, M., (2013), *Study: Millennial Parents Just Like Those From Previous Generations*, available at http://adage.com/article/news/millennials/244523/. Last accessed 13.01.2014.

Munoz, T. (2014) *I would like Scotland to be in control of its own immigration system*, National Collective, available at http://nationalcollective.com/2014/04/28/theresa-munoz-like-scotland-control-immigration-system/. Last accessed 04.04.14.

National Records of Scotland (2014) *Electoral Statistics – Scotland*, available at http://www.gro-scotland.gov.uk/statistics/theme/electoral-stats/10-march-2014/introduction-and-commentary.html. Last accessed 02.05.14.

National Statistics Scotland (October 2013) *SCOTLAND'S POPULATION 2012 The Registrar General's Annual Review of Demographic Trends 158th Edition*, (SG/2013/208), available: http://www.gro-scotland.gov.uk/files2/stats/annual-review-2012/rgar-2012.pdf. Last accessed 04.04.14.

National Theatre of Scotland (2013), *The Great Yes, No, Don't Know 5 Minute Theatre Show,* available at http://fiveminutetheatre.com/. Last accessed 05.05.14.

NUS Scotland (2012) Press Release, available at http://www.nusconnect.org.uk/news/article/priorityscotland/NUS-Scotland-Claim-that-tuition-fees-are-progressive-makes-no-sense/. Last accessed 08.05.14.

Ofcom (2013) *Communications Market Report: Scotland*, available at http://stakeholders.ofcom.org.uk/binaries/research/cmr/cmr13/Scotland_1.pdf. Last accessed 26.06.14.

Office of National Statistics (2014), available at http://www.ons.gov.uk/
ons/datasets-and-tables/index.html. Last accessed 12.04.14

Officer, D., (2014) *100 New Voices of the Independence Generation.*
National Collective, available at http://nationalcollective.
com/2014/02/08/100-new-voices-of-the-independence-generation/.
Last accessed 18.05.14.

O'Shea, A., (2013) *Recognising that the* UK *is a feat of opportunities is
quite possibly something young people do best,* available at http://
bettertogether.net/blog/entry/recognising-that-the-uk-is-a-feast-of-
opportunities-is-quite-possibly-somet. Last accessed 04.01.14.

Peters, M., (2008), Generation Y: Challenging Employers to Provide
Balance, *Family Connections,* 12 (Issue 2)

Prensky, M., (2001), *Digital Natives, Digital Immigrants, From On the
Horizon,* MCB University Press, volume 9, no. 5, also available at
http://www.marcprensky.com/writing/Prensky%20-%20Digital%20
Natives,%20Digital%20Immigrants%20-%20Part1.pdf. Last
accessed 18.05.14.

Ramanathan, S., (2012), *English view of Scottish independence,*
Scottish Times TV, available at https://www.youtube.com/watch?v=_
4jIbpmvOog. Last accessed 08.05.14.

S, Neil, (2014), *Better Together – the positive economic case for the
Union,* available at https://www.youtube.com/watch?v=jJJtIWzJ-
Cos. Last accessed 05.05.14.

Scotland's Census 2011 Shaping our Future (2011), available at http://
www.scotlandscensus.gov.uk/comparator-tool; http://www.scotland-
scensus.gov.uk/ods-analyser/jsf/tableView/crosstabTableView.xhtml.
Last accessed 03.04.14.

Scottish Funding Council (2014) *Higher Eduction Students and
Qualifers at Scottish Institutions 201–13,* available at http://www.
sfc.ac.uk/communications/Statisticalpublications/2014/Higher
EducationStudentsandQualifiersatScottishInstitutions201213.aspx.
Last accessed 08.04.14

Scottish Government, *Action to Support Young People* (2011), available
at http://www.scotland.gov.uk/News/Releases/2011/12/07083420.
Last accessed 04.04.14.

Scottish Government, *Annual Population Survey results for year to 31
December 2013* (2014), available at http://www.scotland.gov.uk/

Topics/Statistics/Browse/Labour-Market/Publications/APSJanDec-Sum. Last accessed 04.04.14.

Scottish Government, Scottish Youth Parliament and Young Scot. (2012) *Scotland's Youth Employment Summit*, available at http://www.youngscot.net/what-we-do/key-documents/scotland%E2%80%99s-youth-employment-summit.aspx. Last accessed 18.05.14.

Scottish Parliament Information Centre (SPICE). (2011) *Scottish Parliament Session 4 Demographics*, p. 4, available at: http://www.scottish.parliament.uk/Annualreportsandaccounts/LG_%282011%29_Paper_046_-_Scottish_Parliament_S4_Demographics.pdf. Last accessed 08.04.14.

Scottish Youth Parliament, (2011), *Change the Picture*, available at http://www.syp.org.uk/img/Youth%20Manifesto/Scottish%20Youth%20Parliament%20Youth%20Manifesto-%20Change%20the%20Picture.pdf. Last accessed 30.04.14

Scottish Youth Parliament. (2012). *The Registration of Civil Partnerships/Same-Sex Marriage – A Consultation Response*, available at http://www.scotland.gov.uk/Resource/0039/00397337.pdf. Last accessed 30.04.14

Scottish Youth Parliament, *Love Equally*, available at http://www.syp.org.uk/love-equally-W21page-485-. Last accessed 18.05.14.

Sheppard, C., (2014) *Open Letter to My Generation*, available at http://nationalcollective.com/2014/01/23/clare-sheppard-an-open-letter-to-my-generation/. Last accessed 08.04.14

Skinner, G. (2014) *State of the Nation*, IPSOS Mori http://www.ipsos-mori.com/researchpublications/researcharchive/3328/State-of-the-Nation-2014.aspx Last accessed 08.04.14

Small, M.; Williamson, K., *et al. Bella Caledonia*, available at http://bellacaledonia.org.uk/. Last accessed 14.04.14.

Sneddon, G., (2014) *100 New Voices of the Independence Generation*, National Collective, available at http://nationalcollective.com/2014/02/08/100-new-voices-of-the-independence-generation/

Stewart, C., (2014)*100 Artists and Creatives who support Independence*. National Collective. Available at http://nationalcollective.com/2014/01/26/100-artists-and-creatives-who-support-scottish-independence/. Last accessed 18.05.14.

Taylor, P.; Keeter, S. (2010), *Millenials Confident. Connected. Open to*

Change, available: http://www.pewsocialtrends.org/files/2010/10/millennials-confident-connected-open-to-change.pdf. Last accessed 09.01.14.

The Guardian (2014). *Generation Y – they're probably no worse than baby-boomers*, available at: http://www.theguardian.com/lifeand-style/shortcuts/2014/mar/16/generation-y-probably-no-worse-than-baby-boomers. Last accessed 08.04.14

The Prince's Trust (2011). *Broke, not Broken: Tackling Youth Poverty and the Aspiration Gap*, available at http://www.princes-trust.org.uk/about_the_trust/what_we_do/research/broke_not_broken.aspx. Last accessed 08.04.14.

Thomason, L. (2014), *I'll be voting yes in September but I wasn't always going to*. National Collective, available at http://nationalcollective.com/2014/04/06/louise-thomason-ill-voting-yes-september-wasnt-always-going/. Last accessed 08.05.14

TNS BMRB (2013). *Scottish Opinion Monitor*, available at (April 2013) http://www.tns-bmrb.co.uk/uploads/files/scottish-independence-data-tables-8-apr-2013_1365519836.pdf; (October 2013) http://www.tns-bmrb.co.uk/uploads/files/som-data-tables-30-october-2013_1383820766.pdf; (December 2013) http://www.tns-bmrb.co.uk/uploads/files/som-data-tables-10-dec-2013_1387291827.pdf

TNS BMRB (2014), Scottish Opinion Monitor. Available at (February 2014) http://www.tnsglobal.com/sites/default/files/whitepaper/TNSUK_SOM%20Data%20Tables_2014Feb19.pdf; (April 2014) http://www.tns-bmrb.co.uk/uploads/files/TNSUK_SOM_DataTables2014Apr16.pdf. Last accessed 18.05.14.

Twenge, J. (2006). *Generation Me*, New York: Simon & Schuster, p. 17.

Westbury, I. (2014) *All Parties need to commit to a plan for young voter engagement*, Democratic Audit UK, available at http://www.democraticaudit.com/?p=2463 Last accessed 08.04.14.

White C., Bruce S., Ritchie J., (2000), *Political Interest and Engagement among Young People*, Joseph Rowntree Foundation, available at http://www.jrf.org.uk/publications/political-interest-and-engagement-among-young-people Last accessed 08.04.14.

YouGov. (March 2012) *Sunday Times Survey Results*, available at http://cdn.yougov.com/cumulus_uploads/document/8xrr8zjqs7/YG-Archives-Pol-ST-results-09-110312.pdf Last accessed 08.04.14.

YouGov. (May 2013), *Sunday Times survey results*, available at http://
cdn.yougov.com/cumulus_uploads/document/lu4hu1in3u/YG-Ar-
chive-Pol-Sunday-Times-results-170513.pdf Last accessed 08.04.14

Young Scot (2014), Scotland's Youth Employment Summit, http://www.
youngscot.net/what-we-do/key-documents/scotland%E2%80%
99s-youth-employment-summit.aspx. Last accessed 04.04.14.

YouthLink Scotland, *Being Young in Scotland* (2009), available at
http://www.youthlinkscotland.org/Index.asp?MainID=10715. Last
accessed 08.04.14.

Resources and Information for Generation ScotY voters:

Better Together Youth http://bettertogether.net/blog/entry/why-become-
a-better-together-youth-rep

Bite the Ballot http://bitetheballot.co.uk/

Generation Yes http://www.generationyes.org/

National Collective http://nationalcollective.com/

NUS Scotland http://www.nus.org.uk/en/nus-scotland/cam-
paigns-in-scotland1/community-network/independence-referendum/

Radical Independence Campaign http://radicalindependence.org/

Scottish Youth Parliament Aye, Naw, Mibbe http://www.ayenawmibbe.
org/

Women for Independence http://www.womenforindependence.org/

Young Scot http://www.youngscot.org/info/161-voting

On Being a Man:
Four Scottish Men in
Conversation

Sandy Campbell, John Carnochan,
Pete Seaman, David Torrance.
Preface by Gerry Hassan
ISBN: 978 1 910021 33 0 PBK £7.99

Men of Scotland, speak up!

*The silences and evasions of too many
men in our society contribute to and
magnify the problems we face in relation
to individual and collective behaviour.*

*Men have to start speaking up as men,
changing themselves and challenging other
men to take responsibility.*
GERRY HASSAN

On Being a Man brings together four
men to consider the condition of
Scottish men, reflect on their own
backgrounds and experiences, and
confront some of the most difficult
issues men face. These include the
changing roles of men in Scottish
society and the role of work and
employment.

What it means to be a man today is
very different from forty years ago: in
terms of expectations, relationships,
how men relate to partners, bring
up children and what constitutes a
modern family. However, there is a
dark side of Scottish masculinity –
seen in the drinking and the violent,
abusive behaviour of some Scots men
and this book addresses this directly,
getting into issues many of us often
shy away from confronting.

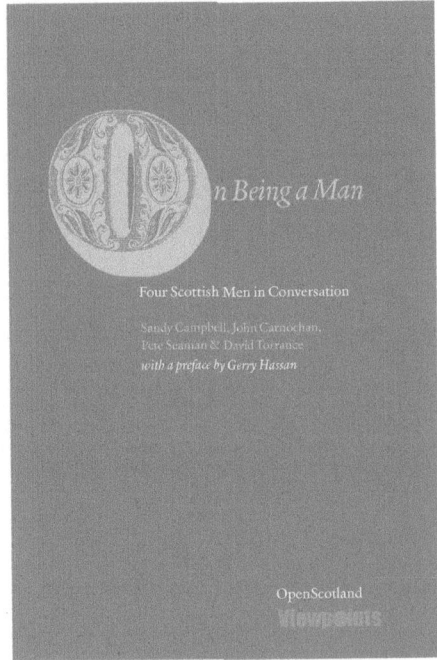

This thoughtful book draws on the
wide-ranging voices of journalist,
writer and broadcaster, David
Torrance; founder of a youth
employment and mentoring charity,
Sandy Campbell; public health
researcher, Pete Seaman; and former
policeman and head of the violence
reduction unit, John Carnochan.

Caledonian Dreaming: The Quest for a Different Scotland

Gerry Hassan

ISBN: 978 1 910021 32 3 PBK £11.99

Caledonian Dreaming: The Quest for a Different Scotland offers a penetrating and original way forward for Scotland beyond the current independence debate. It identifies the myths of modern Scotland, describes what they say and why they need to be seen as myths. Hassan argues that Scotland is already changing, as traditional institutions and power decline and new forces emerge, and outlines a prospectus for Scotland to become more democratic and to embrace radical and far-reaching change.

Hassan drills down to deeper reasons why the many dysfunctions of British democracy could dog an independent Scotland too. With a non-partisan but beady eye on society both sides of the border, in this clever book here are tougher questions to consider than a mere Yes/No.
POLLY TOYNBEE, writer and journalist, *The Guardian*

A brilliant book unpacking the political narratives that have shaped modern Scotland in order to create a space to imagine anew. A book about Scotland important to anyone, anywhere, dreaming a new world.
STEPHEN DUNCOMBE, author

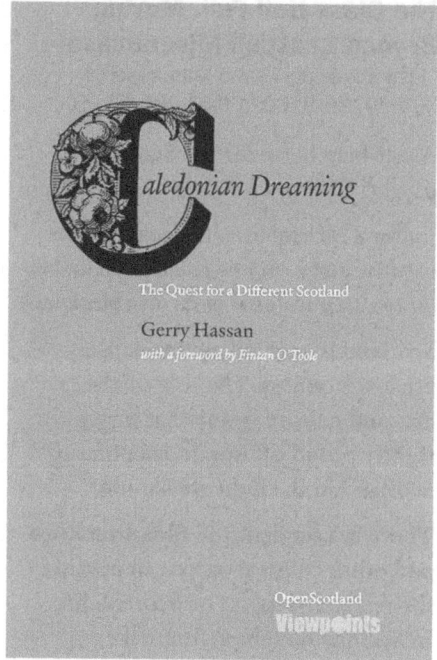

There could be no better harbinger of [...] possibilities than this bracing, searching, discomfiting and ultimately exhilarating book.
FINTAN O'TOOLE

The Glass Half Full: Moving Beyond Scottish Miserabilism

Eleanor Yule and David Manderson
ISBN: 978-1-910021-34-7 PBK £7.99

A self-help book for the Scottish psyche

Cultural Miserablism: the power of the negative story with no redemption and no escape, that wallows in its own bleakness.

Scotland is a small and immensely creative country. The role of the arts and culture is one that many are rightly proud of. But do we portray Scotland in the light we should?

There is a tendency in film, literature and other cultural output to portray the negative aspects of Scottish life. In Seeing Ourselves, filmmaker Eleanor Yule and academic David Manderson explore the origins of this bleak take on Scottish life, its literary and cultural expressions, and how this phenomenon in film has risen to the level of a genre which audiences both domestic and international see as a recognisable story of contemporary Scotland.

What does miserablism tell us about ourselves? When did we become cultural victims? Is it time we move away from an image of Scotland that constantly casts itself as the poor relation?

From the Trainspotting to the Kailyard, Seeing Ourselves confronts the negative Scotland we portray not only to the world but, most importantly, ourselves.

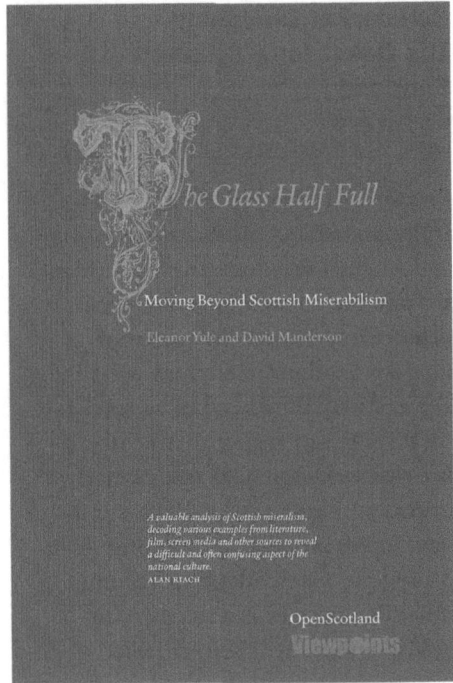

Do [they] *accurately reflect the reality of life in Scotland for the majority of the population or are they just 'stories' we like to tell ourselves about ourselves?*
ELEANOR YULE

Our greatest export is the diversity of our fiction, the myriad of alternatives between its contrasts and all its new heroes and heroines. It's time we knew it.
DAVID MANDERSON

Blossom:
What Scotland Needs to Flourish
Lesley Riddoch
ISBN: 978 1 908373 69 4 PBK £11.99

Weeding out vital components of
Scottish identity from decades of
political and social tangle is no mean
task, but it's one journalist Lesley
Riddoch has undertaken.

Dispensing with the tired, yo-yoing
jousts over fiscal commissions, devo
something-or-other and EU in-or-out,
Blossom pinpoints both the buds of
growth and the blight that's holding
Scotland back. Drawing from its
people and history, as well as the
experience of the Nordic countries
and the author's own passionate
and outspoken perspective, this is
a plain-speaking but incisive call to
restore equality and control to local
communities and let Scotland flourish.

Not so much an intervention in the
independence debate as a heartfelt
manifesto for a better democracy.
THE SCOTSMAN

LESLEY
RIDDOCH

BLOSSOM

What Scotland Needs To Flourish

Viewpoints

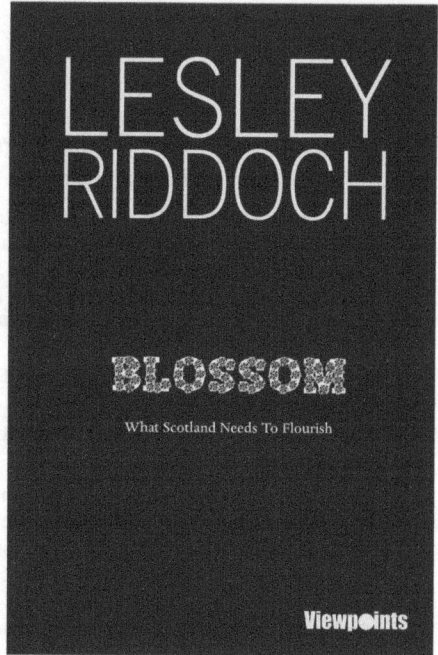

Details of these and other books published by Luath Press can be found at:
www.luath.co.uk

Luath Press Limited

committed to publishing well written books worth reading

LUATH PRESS takes its name from Robert Burns, whose little collie Luath (*Gael.*, swift or nimble) tripped up Jean Armour at a wedding and gave him the chance to speak to the woman who was to be his wife and the abiding love of his life. Burns called one of 'The Twa Dogs' Luath after Cuchullin's hunting dog in Ossian's *Fingal*. Luath Press was established in 1981 in the heart of Burns country, and now resides a few steps up the road from Burns' first lodgings on Edinburgh's Royal Mile.

Luath offers you distinctive writing with a hint of unexpected pleasures.

Most bookshops in the UK, the US, Canada, Australia, New Zealand and parts of Europe either carry our books in stock or can order them for you. To order direct from us, please send a £sterling cheque, postal order, international money order or your credit card details (number, address of cardholder and expiry date) to us at the address below. Please add post and packing as follows: UK – £1.00 per delivery address; overseas surface mail – £2.50 per delivery address; overseas airmail – £3.50 for the first book to each delivery address, plus £1.00 for each additional book by airmail to the same address. If your order is a gift, we will happily enclose your card or message at no extra charge.

ILLUSTRATION: IAN KELLAS

Luath Press Limited
543/2 Castlehill
The Royal Mile
Edinburgh EH1 2ND
Scotland
Telephone: 0131 225 4326 (24 hours)
Fax: 0131 225 4324
email: sales@luath.co.uk
Website: www.luath.co.uk